Out of Joint
7 Thane Works, Thane Villas, London N7 7NU
Tel: 020 7609 0207   Fax: 020 7609 0203
Email: ojo@outofjoint.co.uk
Web: www.outofjoint.co.uk

KEEP IN TOUCH
For information on our shows, tour details and offers, join our **mailing list** (online, or contact details above) letting us know whether you'd like to receive information by post or email. Find us on **Facebook** and follow us on **Twitter** too.

BOOKSHOP
Scripts of many of our previous shows are available at exclusive discounted prices from our online shop:
www.outofjoint.co.uk

EDUCATION
Out of Joint offers a diverse programme of workshops and discussions for groups coming to see our performances. For full details of our education programme, resource packs or Our Country's Good workshops, contact Panda at Out of Joint.

Out of Joint is grateful to the following for their support over the years: Arts Council England, The Foundation for Sport and the Arts, The Granada Foundation, Yorkshire Bank Charitable Trust, The Baring Foundation, The Paul Hamlyn Foundation, The Olivier Foundation, The Peggy Ramsay Foundation, The John S Cohen Foundation, The David Cohen Charitable Trust, The National Lottery through the Arts Council of England, The Prudential Awards, Stephen Evans, Karl Sydow, Harold Stokes and Friends of Theatre, John Lewis Partnership, Unity Theatre Trust, Royal Victoria Hall Foundation. Out of Joint is a Registered Charity No. 1033059

Supported by
**ARTS COUNCIL
ENGLAND**

The Lyric Hammersmith is one of London's leading producing theatres. For over a hundred years, we have welcomed some of the world's finest writers, directors, actors and theatre companies to our stage. From Harold Pinter to Simon Stephens, Sir John Gielgud to Robert Lepage, Complicite to Frantic Assembly. Recent successes have included the terrifying *Ghost Stories*, now playing in the West End at the Duke of York's following its record breaking sell-out run at the Lyric; the multi Olivier award-winning musical *Spring Awakening* which opened at the Lyric in January 2009 before transferring to the West End's Novello Theatre and a groundbreaking adaptation of Kafka's *Metamorphosis* which has toured throughout the world and opens in New York at the Brooklyn Academy of Music in November 2010.

The Lyric creates work that is provoking, entertaining, popular, eclectic, messy, contradictory and diverse. We want to be at the heart of our community as well as being internationally recognised. We celebrate the unique vision of the writer as well as the creative power of collaboration, working with the best theatre artists around as well as encouraging the next generation.

Beautiful theatre, cheap tickets, great pizza and a rooftop garden.

Hammersmith and proud.

Lyric Hammersmith Company

Artistic Director Sean Holmes
Executive Director Jessica Hepburn
PA to the Directors Tracey Woolley

ARTISTIC TEAM
Senior Producer Imogen Kinchin
Director of Young People & Emerging Artists Jennifer Fordham
Producer Bailey Lock
Young People's Producer Hollie Evans
Young People's Producer Rachel Tyson
Creative Youth Worker Nana Bemma
Creative Youth Worker Michelle Masangkay
Assistant to the Artistic Team Sarah Green

ASSOCIATES
Artistic Associates David Baker, Paule Constable, Tashan Cushnie, Ferdy Roberts, Simon Stephens
Pearson Playwright in Residence David Watson

COMMERCIAL SERVICES
Commercial Director James Mackenzie-Blackman
Head of Communications Joanna Down
Marketing Manager Alex Fleming
Commercial Administration Manager Rachel Tattersdill
Marketing Assistant Megan Hall
Strategic Development Associate Adam Coleman
Development Manager: Individual Giving Lyndel Harrison
Development Assistant Becky Turner
Press Manager Amy Belson

THE BIG FELLAH TOUR 2010

CORN EXCHANGE, NEWBURY
Thu 2 – Sat 4 Sep
www.cornexchangenew.com | 01635 522733

ROYAL AND DERNGATE, NORTHAMPTON
Tue 7 – Sat 11 Sep
www.royalandderngate.co.uk | 01604 624811

THEATRE ROYAL, BURY ST EDMUNDS
Tue 14 – Sat 18 Sep
www.theatreroyal.org | 01284 769505

LYRIC HAMMERSMITH, LONDON
Tue 21 Sep – Sat 16 Oct
www.lyric.co.uk | 0871 22 117 22

OXFORD PLAYHOUSE
Tue 19 – Sat 23 Oct
www.oxfordplayhouse.com | 01865 305305

NUFFIELD THEATRE, SOUTHAMPTON
Tue 26 – Sat 30 Oct
www.nuffieldtheatre.co.uk | 023 8067 1771

YORK THEATRE ROYAL
Tue 2 – Sat 6 Nov
www.yorktheatreroyal.co.uk | 01904 623568

BIRMINGHAM REPERTORY THEATRE
Wed 10 – Sat 13 Nov
www.birmingham-rep.co.uk | 0121 236 4455

Out of Joint and the Lyric Hammersmith present

by RICHARD BEAN

First performed on 2 September 2010
at the Corn Exchange, Newbury

out of joint

"You expect something special from Out of Joint"
The Times

Out of Joint is a national and international touring theatre company dedicated to the development and production of new writing. Under the direction of Max Stafford-Clark the company has premiered plays from leading writers including David Hare, Caryl Churchill, David Edgar, Alistair Beaton, Sebastian Barry and Timberlake Wertenbaker, as well as introducing first-time writers such as Simon Bennett, Stella Feehily and Mark Ravenhill.

"Max Stafford-Clark's excellent Out of Joint company"
The Independent

Touring all over the UK, Out of Joint frequently performs at and co-produces with key venues such as the Royal Court and the National Theatre and recently with Sydney Theatre Company. The company has performed in six continents. Back home, Out of Joint also pursues an extensive education programme.

"Out of Joint is out of this world"
Boston Globe

Productions for 2011 include *An Evening with Dr Johnson*, based on the writings of his friend James Boswell; a revival of Caryl Churchill's *Top Girls*; and *The Cameras Have Gone to Other Wars* by Stella Feehily.

Above: *Mixed Up North* (2009) by Robin Soans, photo by Ian Tilton
Below: *Andersen's English* (2010) by Sebastian Barry, photo by Robert Workman

THE COMPANY

Cast (in order of appearance)

David Costello	Finbar Lynch
Ruairi O'Drisceoil	Rory Keenan
Michael Doyle	David Ricardo-Pearce
Karelma	Stephanie Street
Tom Billy Coyle	Youssef Kerkour
Elizabeth Ryan	Claire Rafferty
Frank McArdle	Fred Ridgeway

Director	Max Stafford-Clark
Designer	Tim Shortall
Lighting Designer	Jason Taylor
Sound Designer	Nick Manning
Costume Supervisor	Katie Moore
Associate Director	Blanche McIntyre
Fight Director	Terry King
Dialect Coach	Charmian Hoare

Production Manager	Gary Beestone
Company Stage Manager	Richard Llewelyn
Deputy Stage Manager	Helen Bowen
Assistant Stage Manager	Kitty Stafford-Clark
Re-lighter	Greg Gould

RORY KEENAN
Ruairi O'Drisceoil

Rory has worked primarily on the Dublin stage. Theatre includes the title role in *Hamlet* (Second Age); and the title role in *Macbeth* (Siren). Other work includes *The Importance of Being Earnest* (Gaiety Theatre); *Six Characters In Search Of An Author*, *She Stoops To Folly*, *School For Scandal* and *Saved* (Abbey Theatre); *The Shaughraun* (Albery, West End); *Don Carlos*, and *The Taming Of The Shrew* (Rough Magic); *How He Lied To Her Husband* (Bewleys Theatre); *Sonnets For An Old Century* (X-Bellaire); *A Christmas Carol* and *Festen* (Gate Theatre); *Monged* (Fishamble); *The Drunkard* and *Hysteria* (B*Spoke Theatre Company); *Rich Hall's Levelland* (London and Edinburgh); and *Last Days Of The Celtic Tiger* (Best Supporting Actor, 2008 Irish Times Theatre Awards). Television work includes *Dear Dilemma*, *On Home Ground*, *The Clinic*, and *Showbands* (all RTE); *Aristocrats* (BBC); *Primeval* (ITV) and *Benedict Arnold: A Question Of Honour* (ABC TV). Feature film work includes *Pride And Joy* (Arc Films); *Reign Of Fire* (Disney); *Ella Enchanted* (Miramax); and *Intermission* (Parallel Films). More recently Rory has worked on *Zonad* (Element Films); *One Hundred Mornings* (Blinder Films, due for release in 2010); *The Guard* (Reprisal Films, also due for release later this year).

YOUSSEF KERKOUR
Tom Billy Coyle

Youssef's theatre includes *Comedy of Errors* (Manchester Royal

Exchange); *Mother Courage* (National Theatre); *Thyestes* (Arcola); *All Quiet on the Western Front* (Nottingham Playhouse and tour); *Beast on the Moon* (Nottingham Playhouse); *Mother Courage* (English Touring Theatre); *Titus Andronicus* (Globe Theatre Germany Tour). New York theatre: *Coriolanus* (Division 13); *Journeys Among the Dead* (H.E.R.E); *Maria Del Bosco* (Ontological-Hysteric); *Twelfth Night* (Central Park); *Picasso at the Lapin Agile* (Arden Theatre, Philadelphia); *The Thief's Journal* (Division 13); *Don Giovanni*; *The Magic Flute*; *Ti Jean Blues*. Television includes *The Path to 9/11*, *Oz*, *Holby City*, *The Crusades* and *Upright Citizens Brigade*. Film includes *Infinite Justice*, *Idle Hands*, *Crosseyed*, *American Tale*. Radio: *Silver Street*, *The Eternal Rock*, *You Taught Me To Love Life Father*, *Love My Rifle More Than You* (all BBC Radio).

FINBAR LYNCH
David Costello

Finbar's theatre includes *The Ragged Trousered Philanthropists* (Liverpool Everyman/ Chichester Festival Theatre); *The Fairy Queen* (Opera Comique Paris/Brooklyn Academy of Music); *The Fastest Clock in the Universe* (Hampstead Theatre/Leicester Curve); *Dancing At Lughnasa* (Old Vic Theatre); *Portrait of a Lady*, *A Doll's House*, *Love's Labour's Lost* (Peter Hall Company); *Three Sisters on Hope Street* (Hampstead Theatre and Liverpool Everyman); *The Hothouse*, *Anthony & Cleopatra*, *King Lear* (National Theatre); *Ghosts* (Gate Theatre); *The Tempest*, *A Midsummer Night's Dream*, *Measure for Measure*, *Coriolanus*, *The Alchemist*, *The Virtuoso*, *Amphibians*, *A Woman Killed With Kindness*, *The Two Gentlemen of Verona*

and two productions of *Julius Caesar* (RSC); *As You Desire me* (Playhouse); *The Birthday Party* (Duchess); *Hecuba, To the Green Fields and Beyond, Fool for Love, Translations* (Donmar Warehouse); *Othello* (Greenwich); title role in *Macbeth* (Sheffield Crucible); *Jesus in Messiah* (Riverside UK Tour); *A Moon for the Misbegotten* (Manchester Royal Exchange); *Not About Nightingales* (National Theatre and Broadway, Tony nomination for best supporting actor); *Three Sisters* (Royal Court/Gate Dublin); *Miss Julie* (Greenwich); *Playboy of the Western World* (Abbey, Dublin); *Philadelphia Here I Come, Death of a Salesman, Mass Appeal, Noises Off* (Gaeity, Dublin); *Juno and the Paycock* (Milwaukee Rep); *The Rivals, School for Scandal, Father & Sons, Absurd Person Singular, Les Liaisons Dangereuses, Peer Gynt* (Best Actor, Irish Theatre Awards) (Gate, Dublin). Film appearances include *Matilde, To Kill a King, Lost Battalion, King Lear, Scold's Bridle, The Schooner, The Wild Ponies, A Midsummer Nights Dream.* Finbar has also been involved in major television series including leading roles in *Proof , Mind Games, Small World , Dalziel and Pascoe, Attila the Hun, Holby City, Waking the Dead, Red Cap, Second Sight, Between the Lines, George Gently, Riddlers Moon, The Eejits, Three Wishes for Jamie, Glenroe* and *The Scar.*

CLAIRE RAFFERTY
Elizabeth Ryan

Claire appeared in *Mixed Up North* for Out of Joint and its earlier incarnation *Breaking Barriers in Burnley* at LAMDA. Other theatre includes *Dancing at Lughnasa* (Birmingham Repertory Theatre); *Redundant* (Tinderbox Theatre Company); *Living With Cancer* (Cancer Lifeline); *By the Bog Of Cats* (QUB); *The Trial* (Lyric Theatre Belfast); *The Cherry Orchard* (Theatre at LAMDA). Claire also appeared in the television series *Give my Head Peace* (BBC). Film appearances and voiceovers include *Lovesick* and *Poetry of Abandonment.* Claire received the Norma Award for best Actress.

DAVID RICARDO-PEARCE
Michael Doyle

Theatre includes *Privates on Parade* (WYP and Birmingham Rep); *Saint Joan* (National Theatre); *Ira, The Andes* and *L'Hereux Stratageme* (National Theatre Studio); *The Car Cemetery* (Gate Theatre); *The Hired Man* (Bolton Octagon); *Saturday Night* and *Anyone Can Whistle* (Jermyn Street Theatre & Arts Theatre, West End); *Annie Get Your Gun* (Young Vic); *Inglorious Technicolour* (Stephen Joseph Theatre); *De Monfort* (Orange Tree Theatre); *Two Cities* (Salisbury Playhouse); *A Midsummer Night's Dream* (Bristol Old Vic) and *Sweeney Todd* (Trafalgar Studios/New Ambassadors, West End). Television includes *EastEnders, Outnumbered, Extras* and *Border Crossing* (all for the BBC).

FRED RIDGEWAY
Frank McArdle

Theatre includes *A Comedy Of Errors* (Manchester Royal Exchange); *Edmond* (Wiltons Music Hall); *England People Very Nice* and *The Alchemist* (National Theatre); *The English Game* (Headlong Theatre); *Henry V, Port* (Royal Exchange Manchester); *Coriolanus* (RSC-Stratford then tour); *The Glass Room, My Boy Jack*

(Hampstead Theatre); *In Extremis, Anthony and Cleopatra* (The Globe); *Speaking Like Magpies, Believe What You Will, A New Way To Please you, Thomas More* (RSC - Stratford and West End); *Solid Gold Cadillac* (Garrick/Act Productions); *My Boy Jack* (UK Tour); *Singer* (Oxford Stage Company); *Christmas* (Bush Theatre); *Arms & The Man* (The Touring Partnership); *Absolutely! Perhaps* (Wyndhams); *Outside Edge* (New Vic Theatre); *The Star Throwers* (Stephen Joseph Theatre); *The Weir* (Royal Court Theatre UK Tour); *The Price* (The Bolton Octagon); *Spinning into Butter* (Royal Court Theatre); *Troilus and Cressida* (Tour & Old Vic); *The Rise and Fall Of Little Voice* (Everyman Theatre, Liverpool); *The Imposter* (Plymouth Theatre Royal); *LOOT* (West End); *LOOT* and *Saturday, Sunday, Monday* (Chichester Festival Theatre); *Dealer's Choice* (West Yorkshire Playhouse); *The Alchemist, Swamp City* (Birmingham Rep). Film appearances include *Kapital, Shadow Observers, Memorabilis, The Kinky Boot Factory, Monk Dawson*, and *A Twist In the Tail*. Television includes *The Bill, Heartbeat, Doctors, My Boy Jack, The Verdict, Trial and Retribution, Casualty, Spooks II, The Royal, EastEnders, Inspector Lynley Mysteries-For the Sake Of Elena, The Bill, Peak Practice, Never Never, Midsomer Murders, Small Potatoes, Heartbeat*, and *Father Ted*.

STEPHANIE STREET
Karelma

Stephanie trained at LAMDA. She appeared in *Mixed Up North* for Out of Joint. Recently she wrote and performed in *Sisters* at the Sheffield Crucible. Other theatre includes *The Contingency Plan* (Bush Theatre); *Shades* (Royal Court);*The Scarecrow and his Servant* (Southwark Theatre); *Sweet Cider*

(Arcola Theatre); *Not the End of the World* (Bristol Old Vic); *Too Close to Home* (Lyric Hammersmith); *The Laramie Project* (Kit Productions) and a UK tour of *The Vagina Monologues*. Television work includes *Hens, On Expenses, Holby City, EastEnders, Soundproof, Monday Monday, Apparitions, Never Better, Primeval, The Commander III, Nylon, Twenty Things to do Before You're Thirty* and *Red Cap*. Stephanie has also just filmed *Attack The Block* directed by Joe Cornish.

RICHARD BEAN

Richard Bean's plays include *Toast* (National Theatre/Royal Court); *Mr England* (National Theatre and Sheffield Crucible); *The Mentalists* (Lyttleton Loft, National Theatre); *Under The Whaleback* (Royal Court, winner of the George Devine Award); *Smack Family Robinson* (Newcastle Live); *The God Botherers* (Bush Theatre); *Honeymoon Suite* (Royal Court and English Touring Theatre, winner of the Pearson Play of the Year Award); *Harvest* (Royal Court, winner of the Critics' Circle Award for Best Play); a version of Moliere's *The Hypochondriac* (Almeida); *Up on Roof* (Hull Truck); *The English Game* (Headlong); *England People Very Nice* (National Theatre, nominated for the Best New Comedy Olivier); *Pub Quiz is Life* (Hull Truck) and, as a co-writer, *Jack and the Beanstalk* (Lyric Hammersmith). His radio plays include *Of Rats and Men, Yesterday, Unsinkable* and *Robin Hood's Revenge*.

GRAHAM COWLEY
Producer

Out of Joint's Producer since 1998. His long collaboration with Max Stafford-Clark began as Joint Stock Theatre Group's first General Manager for seven years in the 1970s. He was General Manager of the Royal Court for eight years, and on their behalf transferred a string of hit plays to the West End. His career has spanned the full range of theatre production, from small fringe companies to major West End shows and large scale commercial tours. Outside Out of Joint, he has translated Véronique Olmi's *End of Story* (Chelsea Theatre) and has produced the 'Forgotten Voices from the Great War' series of plays including *What the Women Did* (Southwark Playhouse, 2004); *Red Night* by James Lansdale Hodson (Finborough, 2005) and *My Real War 1914-?*, based on the letters of a young WW1 soldier, which toured twice in 2007 and played at Trafalgar Studios in October 2009.

NICK MANNING
Sound Designer

Nick is Head of Sound at the Lyric Hammersmith. For the Lyric: *Ghost Stories* (also at Duke of York's); *Three Sisters*, *Jack and the Beanstalk*, *Comedians*, *The Jitterbug Blitz*, *Hang On*, *Cinderella*, *Spyski!*, *Depth Charge*, *Love – the Musical*, *The Birthday Party*, *The Resistible Rise of Arturo Ui*, *Beauty and the Beast*, *Accidental Heroes*, *Absolute Beginners*, *Ramayana*, *Metamorphosis*, *Too Close to Home*, *The Odyssey*, *Some Girls Are Bigger Than Others*, *The Firework-Maker's Daughter*, *Don Juan*, *Oliver Twist*, *Pericles*, *Camille*, *A Christmas Carol*, *The Prince of Homburg*, *Aladdin*, *The Servant* and *Pinocchio*. Other theatre includes *Gizmo Love*, *Excuses*, *Out of Our Heads* (ATC); *The Unsinkable Clerk* (Network of Stuff); *Grumpy Old Women 2*, *Britt on Britt*, *Grumpy Old Women* (Avalon); *Airsick*, *Crooked*, *When You Cure Me* (Bush); *Darwin in Malibu* (Hampstead); *The Master and Margarita* (National Youth Theatre); *Rabbit* (Frantic Assembly) and *Great Expectations* (Bristol Old Vic).

BLANCHE McINTYRE
Associate Director

Directing includes *Molière, or The League of Hypocrites* (Finborough); *Birds* (Southwark Playhouse); *The Revenger's Tragedy* (BAC); *Wuthering Heights* (National Tour); *A Model For Mankind* (Cock Tavern); *Three Hours After Marriage* (Union Theatre); *Doctor Faustus*, *The Devil Is An Ass* and *The Strange Case of Dr Jekyll and Mr Hyde as told to Carl Jung by an Inmate of Broadmoor Asylum* (White Bear Theatre); *Cressida*, *The Invention of Love* (Edinburgh Fringe); *The Master and Margarita* (Greenwich Playhouse); *Prometheus Bound* (Burton Taylor Theatre). Film: *Lost Hearts*. Assistant directing includes *Can't Pay? Won't Pay!* and *Meetings* (Arcola Theatre); *Aladdin* (Oxford Playhouse); *Charlie and Henry* (New End Theatre) and *The Taming Of The Shrew*, *The Beggar's Opera*, *Macbeth* and *The Importance of Being Earnest* (Changeling Theatre). Associate directing: *A Midsummer Night's Dream*, *The Merry Wives of Windsor* (Changeling Theatre). Blanche was the first winner of the Leverhulme Bursary for Emerging Theatre Directors in 2009, and was Director in Residence at the National Theatre Studio and the Finborough Theatre in 2009.

TIM SHORTALL
Designer

For Out of Joint Tim designed *The Overwhelming* (also at the National Theatre and Laura Pels Theatre New York) and *King of Hearts* (also at Hampstead Theatre). Productions at the Lyric Hammersmith include *900 Oneonta*, *What You Get And What You Expect* and *Eugene Onegin*. Current theatre includes *La Cage Aux Folles* on Broadway (2010 Tony Nomination Best Design of a Musical) and previously at the Playhouse Theatre; the Menier Chocolate Factory production of *Sweet Charity* at the Theatre Royal Haymarket and recently Trevor Griffith's epic *A New World – The Life of Thomas Paine* at Shakespeare's Globe. Other theatre includes *The Philanthropist* (Donmar Warehouse and Broadway); *Awake and Sing* (Almeida); *See How They Run* (Duchess) and several productions with Terry Johnson: *Rookery Nook* (Menier Chocolate Factory); *Whipping It Up* (Ambassadors) and *Elton John's Glasses* (Queens Theatre); Other London work includes *Telstar*, *Body and Soul*, *Murder By Misadventure*, *The Cooks Tour*; costumes for *The Big Knife*; *Excuses*, *Haunted*, *The Amen Corner*, *900 Oneonta* (Old Vic) and *Disappeared* (Royal Court). Tim has designed for most of the major regional theatres in the UK and highlights include *Privates On Parade*, *The Colonel Bird* and *Broken Glass* (all for Rupert Goold); *Single Spies* and *Having A Ball* for David Grindley and *Roots* (Barclays TMA Award nomination for Best Design). Designs for dance include *Private City/Track and Field* (Sadler's Wells Royal Ballet); *Sonata In Time* (Scottish Ballet); *Rhyme Nor Reason* and *Party Game* (Norwegian National Ballet); *The Nightingale* (Dutch National Ballet) and *Uncertain Steps* (Introdans Holland and Ontario Ballet Theatre). Television work includes *20ᵗʰ Century Blues: a tribute to Noel Coward* with Robbie Williams and Elton John (BBC) and *The Nightingale* (NOS Dutch TV) which was the Netherlands' entry in the Prix Italia and won the RAI Prize for Best Design.

MAX STAFFORD-CLARK
Director

Educated at Trinity College, Dublin, Max Stafford-Clark co-founded Joint Stock Theatre Group in 1974 following his Artistic Directorship of The Traverse Theatre, Edinburgh. From 1979 to 1993 he was Artistic Director of The Royal Court Theatre. In 1993 he founded the touring company, Out of Joint. His work as a Director has overwhelmingly been with new writing, and he has commissioned and directed first productions by many leading writers, including Sue Townsend, Stephen Jeffreys, Timberlake Wertenbaker, Sebastian Barry, April de Angelis, Mark Ravenhill, Andrea Dunbar, Robin Soans, Alistair Beaton, Stella Feehily, David Hare and Caryl Churchill. In addition he has directed classic texts including *The Seagull*, *The Recruiting Officer* and *King Lear* for the Royal Court; *A Jovial Crew*, *The Wives' Excuse* and *The Country Wife* for the Royal Shakespeare Company; and *The Man of Mode*, *She Stoops to Conquer*, *Three Sisters* and *Macbeth* for Out of Joint. He directed David Hare's *The Breath of Life* for Sydney Theatre Company in 2003. Academic credits include an honorary doctorate from Oxford Brookes University, an honorary doctorate from Warwick University and visiting Professorships at the Universities of Hertfordshire, Warwick and York. His books are *Letters to George, Taking Stock* and *Our Country's Good: Page To Stage*.

JASON TAYLOR
Lighting Designer

Recent designs include *The Empire* (Royal Court); *Six Degrees of Separation* (Old Vic); *Duet for One* (Almeida/Vaudeville Theatre); *Rum and Coca Cola* (ETT Tour); *Awaking Beauty* (Scarborough); *Rainman* (Apollo); *Flashdance* (national tour); *Blackbird* (national tour); *Year Of The Rat* (West Yorkshire Playhouse); *Pygmalion* (Broadway); Peter Hall Season (Bath); *Journey's End* (Broadway- Tony Nomination For Best Lighting Design); *Absurd Person Singular* (Garrick); *The Letter* (Wyndhams); *How The Other Half Loves* (national tour); *Entertaining Angels* (Chichester Festival Theatre and national tour): *BCC* (National Theatre); *Honour* (Wyndhams); *What The Butler*

Saw (Criterion); *Glorious* (Duchess and Birmingham Rep); *The God of Hell* (Donmar Warehouse); *Some Girl* (Gielgud); *National Anthems* (Old Vic); *Twelfth Night* (Albery); *Journey's End* (Comedy, Duke Of York's and national tour); *High Society* (Shaftesbury); *The Lady in the Van* (national tour); *Madness of George III* (West Yorkshire Playhouse); *Us and Them*, *The Dead Eye Boy* (Hampstead Theatre); *Abigail's Party* (New Ambassadors/Whitehall/national tour); *Pretending to be Me* (Comedy); *Little Shop of Horrors* (West Yorkshire Playhouse); *The Clearing* (Shared Experience); *Single Spies* (national tour); *Pirates Of Penzance* (national tour); *Office* (Edinburgh International Festival); and *Iolanthe*, *The Mikado* and *Yeoman Of The Guard* (Savoy). Jason has lit over 300 other productions including: 20 seasons at the Open Air Theatre, Regents Park; *Kindertransport* (Vaudeville); *Rosencrantz and Guildenstern are Dead* (Piccadilly); *And Then There Were None* (Duke Of York's); *Great Balls Of Fire* (Cambridge) and other productions at the Bush, Hampstead and The Bridewell and numerous productions for Soho Theatre. Jason has also designed at most major regional theatres including Nottingham, Sheffield, Plymouth, West Yorkshire Playhouse, Birmingham, Edinburgh, Southampton, Clwyd and Liverpool.

Thanks to Blair Staynings for the paintings.

The Troubles - a Chronology

This chronology is necessarily brief. The 3,500 people killed in "the Troubles" since 1969 cannot be mentioned individually nor can the circumstances be explained in detail. Some incidents mentioned below only warrant inclusion because they are relevant to the play.

1170	The first English invasion of Ireland.
1541	Henry VIII declares himself to be King of Ireland.
1690	Battle of the Boyne fought on Ireland's East Coast between the Catholic King James and the Protestant King William. The latter won, and the battle is commemorated annually by Orange Order marches, or "walks".
1798	Wolfe Tone's united Irishmen defeated. Wolfe Tone imprisoned and slits his own throat. He is buried in Bodenstown, Co Kildare which became an annual pilgrimage for Republicans.
1801	United Kingdom created through Act of Union including Ireland.
1916	Easter Rising defeated.
1921-23	Irish civil war. Michael Collins (the Big Fellah) killed. Northern Ireland created.
1939	IRA bombing campaign in England.
1966	Ulster Volunteer Force (UVF) formed in Belfast.
1968	Civil Rights marches in Northern Ireland.
1969	British Army arrive in Northern Ireland.
	IRA splits. Provisional IRA (PIRA) formed.
	The Irish Northern Aid Committee (Noraid) is established in the USA, ostensibly to raise money for PIRA prisoners' families.
	George Harrison begins running Mafia guns to the IRA from his base in New York.
1971	First British soldier shot dead.

1972	Bloody Sunday. British Paratroopers fired on a civil rights march in Derry. 13 died, and a 14th died later as a result of injuries. The Saville Inquiry concluded (in 2010) that all had been unarmed. Bloody Sunday was followed by a swell in support for the Republican cause, and an increase in IRA membership.
	Bombing campaign in England and Northern Ireland.
	PIRA leaders have talks in Libya.
1974	M62 coach bombing. Nine British soldiers and three civilians killed.
	Birmingham pub bombings. Twenty one civilians killed.
1976	Six Catholic civilians killed by loyalists.
	Kingsmill massacre. Ten protestants killed by Republican faction.
1977	Cellular (small group) structure of IRA introduced.
1978	Martin McGuinness appointed PIRA chief.
1980	Republican prisoners begin a hunger strike in the Maze prison.
1980	Joe Doherty arrested as part of a hit squad that kills SAS officer.
1981	Bobby Sands, a hunger striker, elected to the UK Parliament while in prison. Later that year, he dies, as do a further nine hunger strikers.
	Joe Doherty and seven others escape from the Crumlin Road jail. Doherty travels on to New York where he starts work as a barman.
	Qaddafi showers PIRA with cash.
	Christin ni Elias avoids being assassinated by her own PIRA colleagues following an "affair" with a British intelligence officer. Escapes to Canada.
1982	Gerry Adams increasingly prominent in Sinn Fein, publicly distancing himself from the IRA. Elected to Northern Ireland Assembly.

1983	Adams elected to Westminster Parliament as an abstaining MP for West Belfast.
	Adams becomes president of Sinn Fein.
	Harrods bombed. Six people are killed.
	The racehorse Shergar is "kidnapped" by the PIRA. It is believed to have been shot very shortly after its abduction from stables.
1984	Big PIRA arms deal negotiated with Libya.
	New York Irish Emerald Society Police Band play in the parade at Bundoran, County Donegal, to commemorate the deaths of 10 republican hunger strikers.
1985	Anglo Irish agreement signed, giving the Irish Government an advisory role in Northern Ireland's government and setting out conditions for the establishment of a devolved government for the region.
	The fishing boat "Casamara" makes two trips bringing arms from Libya.
	Boston Police Department flak jackets are found in a PIRA shipment of arms from America on the trawler Valhalla.
1986	The "Kula" lands 14 tons of arms from Libya.
	The "Villa" lands 105 tons of arms and semtex from Libya.
1987	Inside intelligence leads to the arrest of the trawler "Eksund" carrying arms from Libya.
	PIRA bomb kills eleven on Remembrance Day at Enniskillen cenotaph. Gordon Wilson, father of Marie Wilson, one of the victims, expresses forgiveness to the killers.
1988	Three PIRA operatives killed in Gibraltar.
1990	Gerry Adams working to separate Sinn Fein and PIRA.
	PIRA's first use of human bombs i.e. bombs, tied to PIRA prisoners, and driven at troops.
	Joe Doherty becomes a cause célèbre in New York and 130 Congressmen back his claim to be a political prisoner. A street corner in New York is named Doherty corner.

1992	Adams loses his West Belfast seat to the SDLP (Social Democratic and Labour Party).
1995	Gerry Adams attends a reception at the White House at the invitation of Bill Clinton.
1996	PIRA bomb London docklands, killing two people. Manchester bombed: 212 people are injured though no one is killed.
1997	Real IRA formed.
1998	Good Friday Agreement reached, Northern Ireland Assembly created.
	Real IRA bomb Omagh town centre, killing 29 people.
1999	Martin McGuinness becomes Minister for Education in the Northern Ireland Assembly.
2001	9/11 attacks on the twin towers of the World Trade Centre in New York.
	George W Bush commits the USA to a war against terrorism.
	John McDonagh, chairman of the New York Irish Freedom Committee says "we've got a sponsored five mile fun run in October and a dinner dance in January, so we'll wait and see if the take is down."
2002	Assembly suspended.
2007	Power-sharing Assembly reinstated with Ian Paisley as First Minister and Martin McGuinness as Deputy First Minister.
2010	Department of Justice founded on transfer of powers of justice and policing to the Northern Ireland Executive.
	Real IRA plant car bomb near MI5's Northern Ireland base. No-one killed.

THE BIG FELLAH

Richard Bean

THE BIG FELLAH

OBERON BOOKS
LONDON

First published in 2010 by Oberon Books Ltd
521 Caledonian Road, London N7 9RH
Tel: 020 7607 3637 / Fax: 020 7607 3629
e-mail: info@oberonbooks.com
www.oberonbooks.com

A catalogue record for this book is available from the British
Library.

ISBN: 978-1-84002-775-4

Cover image by Dan O'Flynn/Alamy

Printed in Great Britain by CPI Antony Rowe, Chippenham.

Set / Staging

Most of the action takes place in an apartment in the Woodlawn district of the Bronx.

Other locations are Costello's speeches at St. Patrick's Day dinners, and the art gallery settings for Ruairi's meetings with Karelma. Both these can be done without fixed staging.

The apartment is formed out of the first floor of an old brownstone. It's a man's place and generally cramped, lacking style, and scruffy. There is a kitchen/diner/reception type arrangement. Stage right and in the back wall are four doors, three to bedrooms, and one to a bathroom. The entrance to the apartment is stage left. A big sash window stage left looks out on to 237th street. On one of the walls an acoustic guitar hangs as a decoration. An old two seater sofa, an armchair, and coffee table, fill the space. Some sporting trophies - baseball and/or ice hockey, maybe a team photo with a young Michael. One or two posters of rock bands of the sixties and a big bad landscape, redolent of a romanticised Ireland.

Through the different time periods the apartment furniture might change with fashions, as well as predictable updates of the domestic technology.

Characters

DAVID COSTELLO
37 in 1972

MICHAEL DOYLE
20s in 1972

RUAIRI O'DRISCEOIL
20s in 1972

TOM BILLY COYLE
20s in 1972

KARELMA
20s in 1972

ELIZABETH RYAN
30s in 1981

FRANK MCARDLE
50s in 1987

Prologue

(1972. DAVID COSTELLO is isolated in a spot. A surround soundscape of chatter, eating, cutlery/crockery clanging. The audience is the St. Patrick's day parade dinner crowd. COSTELLO is dressed in a full Brian Boru and Irish kilt. He lights a cigar. He's cool. He's done this before. He picks up a wine glass and taps it with a fork. This has no effect on the chatter which continues with only a few shushes thrown in. He tries again with the wine glass. No change. He looks stage left and mimes a blow on the pipes. There is an almighty and comic blast on the pipes, rather longer than COSTELLO wanted. It is followed by laughter and applause. He speaks in a New York accent.)

COSTELLO: I won't keep you long. I understand that one of you's godda go to work in the morning.

(Laughter.)

I'd like to thank the chef, Jimmy Schultz, and all his staff for a real terrific meal – as ever!

(Applause.)

Hell! At five hundred dollars a plate – it's godda be good!

(Laughter.)

It woulda been a lot cheaper if we'd all been born Protestant!

(Laughter.)

THE FIRST EVER NEW YORK ST.PATRICK'S DAY PARADE WAS IN 1766!

(Small cheer.)

In nineteen seventy two, two hundred and six years later, WE'RE STILL MARCHING!

(Many cheers.)

America has given each of us the opportunity to fulfil our true potential!

God Bless America!

ALL: God Bless America!

COSTELLO: Some of us have prospered.

(Laughter. Costello acknowledges that the laughter is directed at him.)

And America asks only one thing of us – that we become Americans. I am an American …AND, I am Irish!

(Cheers. COSTELLO is in tears.) This year, the parade, this dinner, it feels different. Just over a month ago, in Derry, thirteen unarmed Irishmen were murdered in cold blood by foreign soldiers!

(Grumbles of disgust.) I fought one war for America. Korea. Many of you have sons in Vietnam. I killed men, men I did not know, men who would have killed me had I not killed them. And I'd do it again if my nation asked me to.

(He gets out a handkerchief and wipes his tear filled eyes.)

I really do not know if these wars in Asia are just wars – this guy… whatshisname…Chomsky thinks they're not, but I didn't see him over there

(Laughter.) War is hell! But more disgusting than war is tyranny. Our black American brothers in the Civil Rights movement have finally removed the stain of racial discrimination from this nation and yet today our Irish Catholic men and women exist only as targets in the cross hairs of the British rifles.

(Supportive grumbles.)

Kissinger and Nixon, I make no apologies for putting them in that order

(Laughter.) – they got one eye on the Soviet Union, one eye on Vietnam, and one eye on the moon!

(Laughter.) If my math is correct – they got one good eye left!

(Laughter.) Look to Ireland Mr. Kissinger! Look to your "ancestral home" Mr. President!

(Laughter.) There's forty million Irish Americans ready to back you for a second term if you do the right thing!

(Cheers.) What is the right thing? I know what it ain't! It ain't détente. Was it détente when my father, and four hundred thousand of his American buddies died kicking the Nazis outa France!? No! Do the right thing!

(Applause.)

OK, OK, I'm not calling for a beach landing in Galway.

(Laughter.)

But take the reins off of our money!

(Yeah!) Quit supplying arms to the Brits!

(Yeah!) And Kissinger, stick your détente up your derrière, and get your German ass over to London with this message – "No direct rule, Brits out!". *(Cheers.)* Our struggle for freedom needs money. Earlier today, the police, the firemen, the longshoremen, the Irish workers who keep this great city alive filled the buckets on the parade with hard earned dollars and quarters. But from you guys – the blessed sons of Ireland in America – I don't want five dollar bills, I don't want ten dollar bills. I want cheques!

> *(Laughter.)* "For freedom comes from God's right hand
> And needs a Godly train
> And <u>WEALTHY</u> men must make our land
> *(Knowing Laughter.)* A nation once again!"

(Huge cheering.)

To black.

Act 1

SCENE 1

(Sunday March 19th 1972. It's mid morning. The Woodlawn apartment in the Bronx. Lots of plastic decorated with amateurishly painted shamrocks. Ruairi is diallng a number on the phone. He is an Irishman of about 28. He is wearing only underpants, and a vest. He talks with a strong Cork accent.)

RUAIRI: *(On the phone, talking secretively.)* It's me…ME!…that fireman's place. Yous can check out the apartment, and him, kill two birds with the one stone… I am not getting on the number 4 train in the Bronx wi' eighteen buckets full o' fucking money!… Mr Costello, Jesus! There's so much money I'VE GOT A FUCKING HARD ON! …Sh!

> *(A noise from the other bedroom as MICHAEL rolls out of bed yawning and groaning.)*

… see…yer've woken him up now wi' yer shouting… …Two forty seven and Martha, …apartment 4, number 87, … it'll only tek yer five minutes. Big ugly fucking brownstone…see yous.

> *(RUAIRI puts the phone down. He opens the curtains. MICHAEL comes out of his room. He is suffering from a hangover. He is a young, well built man of about 25. He wears pyjama bottoms and a singlet. He speaks in a blue collar New York accent without a hint of Irish.)*

RUAIRI: Yer look as sick as a small hospital.

MICHAEL: Yeah.

RUAIRI: It must be hard work living in this bit of the Bronx.

MICHAEL: The blacks?

RUAIRI: The "Oirish". Woodlawn reminds me of the very worst bit of Tipperary. I bet if yer go in that church there they'll have a statue of the Virgin Mary weeping blood every Easter, and a priest tryna fuck the kids.

MICHAEL: What's the weather like?

RUAIRI: Soft.

(During the next MICHAEL makes coffee using a Bialetti.)

Yer not that Irish are yer Michael?

MICHAEL: No.

RUAIRI: A true born Irishman would know what I meant by "soft". Soft rain. But yer didn't know what the fuck I was talking about did yer?

MICHAEL: No.

RUAIRI: And yer awful laconic fer an Irishman with yer little "No" here and a little "No" there. Have yer got a sister called Mary?

MICHAEL: No.

RUAIRI: Yer not Irish then. But there's hope yet – yer've got a guitar. Do yer play?

MICHAEL: No.

RUAIRI: Good. I fucking hate Irish music. The worst song in the world is that Johnny O'Leary song – "The Hair Fell Off Me Coconut"? Do you know it?

MICHAEL: No.

RUAIRI: *(Singing.)* Oh the hair fell off me coconut
The hair fell off me coconut
Oh the hair fell off me coconut
And how do you like it baldy?
I'm a Pink Floyd man meself.

(RUAIRI has his hands on the guitar and pulls at it but it's nailed to the wall.)

RUAIRI: -Yer've nailed a musical instrument to the wall so! Frank McArdle, he'd kill yer for less.

MICHAEL: Who's Frank McArdle?

RUAIRI: South Armagh alcoholic. I was in the Kesh with him. For this, Frank, he'd blindfold yer, drill yer kneecaps, beat yer till yer were lard, set fire to the lard, and then piss on yer to put yer out, so's he could beat yer, and light yer up, all over again. He's a big music lover yer see.

MICHAEL: It's my grandfather's. He was from Omey Island near Clifden.

RUAIRI: I've won good money on them sands on board some of Ireland's finest horses.

MICHAEL: You were a jockey?

RUAIRI: What the fuck else are yer gonna do with a little Irishman wi' no schoolin'?

MICHAEL: Tom Billy said your brother could sell me a plot of land in Ireland.

RUAIRI: I'll sell yer a bit of Omey Island itself. And it'll be a practical purchase. A little strip, three by six.

MICHAEL: How many acres is that?

RUAIRI: Three fucking <u>foot</u> that way, and six fucking <u>foot</u> that way. Yer get the six by three bit of Omey Island, a stone, and the coffin itself. Five hundred dollars deposit, and then when you can, another coupla grand.

MICHAEL: Two thousand bucks?!

RUAIRI: Yer get to fly Aer Lingus – first class.

MICHAEL: But what's the point, I'd be dead?

RUAIRI: You're not a believer then?

MICHAEL: No.

RUAIRI: Get dressed. The Big Fellah's on his way.

MICHAEL: Is he gonna tell you where they're sending you?

RUAIRI: Ah, there's no debate, it'll be Canada, and I fucking hate Canada. All that wild open space, and not been able to move fer fucking moose shit.

MICHAEL: I didn't know you'd been?

RUAIRI: I seen it on the telly. I'll be dead in a week, you watch. Eaten alive by beavers.

(RUAIRI busies himself with the buckets. Enter KARELMA. She is an attractive Puerto Rican of about 25. She is wearing only a T shirt and knickers.)

KARELMA: Hiya guys.

MICHAEL: Michael Doyle. It's my apartment.

KARELMA: Karelma. Good morning Ruairi.

RUAIRI: *(Sulking.)* Yeah.

(KARELMA checks out the buckets full of money.)

KARELMA: So does this money go to the IRA?

RUAIRI: Fuck no! What makes yer think I would be involved with them thieving, murdering, bandits?

KARELMA: Cos last night, in the bar, you told me that you were on the run, busted outa some jail in Ireland by the IRA and had been lying low in New York for six months waiting to get smuggled into Canada by the IRA.

RUAIRI: *(Laughing.)* Now, any man, after a few drinks, might make up a white lie like that if he thinks there might be a fuck in it. Michael, you're a fireman, I bet you exaggerate about how many cats yer've rescued, if yer chatting up a lovely looking cat lover.

MICHAEL: Ruairi saying that he's in the IRA is conclusive proof that he's not in the IRA.

RUAIRI: No true member of the IRA would be that stupid.

KARELMA: Pulling pints in an Irish bar on parade night is a weird take on "lying low".

RUAIRI: I was wearing a wig.

KARELMA: A green wig. Can I use your bathroom Michael?

MICHAEL: Sure. This one here.

(MICHAEL opens the door for her, she goes in.)

MICHAEL: *(Whispering.)* She's really hot.

RUAIRI: Ah, I coulda flahed the arse of her if she'd a let me. Must be a lesbian.

(Intercom sounds. MICHAEL goes to it.)

MICHAEL: Yeah?

TOM BILLY: *(Distort.)* Coyle!

(MICHAEL buzzes to let him in.)

MICHAEL: Coyle – with their buckets.

(RUAIRI goes to look out the window.)

MICHAEL: If it isn't Canada, you could stay here, ya know, three bedrooms is too big for me on my own. If Costello OKs it for the safe house, and pays a retainer, then you can have one of the rooms.

RUAIRI: I'm sick o' me brother's for sure.

(Enter TOM BILLY. He is about 25. He's wearing full NYPD uniform. He is carrying a pile of buckets, which he hands over, and two NYPD flak jackets.)

TOM BILLY: There's a couple of faggots out there on your sidewalk man. Holding hands. Men. Holding hands. In America.

MICHAEL: Yeah?

TOM BILLY: Fucking spic and a fucking brick top white guy. Thank Christ there ain't a single fucking womb between them. Where d'yer want these buckets man?

MICHAEL: Here.

(MICHAEL takes the buckets off TOM BILLY.)

RUAIRI: What's that other lump o' stuff yer got there?

TOM BILLY: Flak jackets.

(TOM BILLY gives them to RUAIRI.)

RUAIRI: I see it's left to me to paint over the lettering is it?

TOM BILLY: Hey! The Big Fellah said they wan' a coupla flak jackets. I get two fucking flak jackets. All of a sudden I'm a the fuck up!

RUAIRI: Turn yer amplifier down yer big noisy langer!

MICHAEL: We got company.

(RUAIRI heads off down the corridor and slings the flak jackets into a room.)

TOM BILLY: I godda gig tonight? Comedy Kitchen, West Third and Bleeker. Open Mike. Ten Minutes.

MICHAEL: Sorry man, I got a shift.

TOM BILLY: Bullshit!

(TOM BILLY grabs him round the neck and playfully squeezes him.)

MICHAEL: Agh! Easy man!

TOM BILLY: Ruairi?

RUAIRI: Yer've not got a funny bone in yer body, and I say that as a good friend.

TOM BILLY: Fuck you!

MICHAEL: Don't do the nigger material man.

TOM BILLY: Why not?

(*KARELMA enters from the bathroom.*)

KARELMA: (*To COYLE.*) Hi?

MICHAEL: Karelma, this is Officer Coyle.

KARELMA: Coyle, Doyle, cop, fireman. You've got pretty broad horizons Michael?

TOM BILLY: Are you bullshiting me?! If you're not legal I'm gonna run your pretty ass outa town.

KARELMA: (*Indicating RUAIRI.*) He's the IRA killer man, you're the New York cop. Why don't you run him outa town?

TOM BILLY: Excuse me lady, are you slandering the character of this gentleman?

MICHAEL: Cut her some slack Tom Billy!

(*TOM BILLY moves towards the door.*)

TOM BILLY: You don't exist lady! I'm outa here. Comedy Kitchen, West –

RUAIRI: – Fuck off!

(*RUAIRI slams the door on him.*)

MICHAEL: Are you illegal?

KARELMA: I'm as American as you man.

(*KARELMA rolls a joint. During the next she lights it, smokes it and passes it on to MICHAEL.*)

Your "nation" is your head, yeah. I believe in freedom. So I'm here. In America. You're Irish, Rory, what do the Irish nation believe in?

RUAIRI: Drinking, singing, and some of them do a bit of cow farming.

KARELMA: Puerto Ricans wanna be Americans.

RUAIRI: They invaded yer fucking country! I'm glad yer wouldn't let me fuck yer last night. Why would I want to fuck an idiot!

KARELMA: Everywhere in the world has been invaded man! Here too. Manhattan Island was stolen from the Wappinger Indian nation.

RUAIRI: They sat down with that Dutch fellah and agreed a price!

KARELMA: Sixty motherfucking guilders worth of trinkets. For the whole of Manhattan Island.

RUAIRI: They didn't live here all the time.

KARELMA: I'm sooo glad I didn't fuck you last night. Why would I want to fuck an idiot?

(MICHAEL starts sorting money, not counting it. ie: putting notes of equal denominations in piles.)

RUAIRI: Yer like him don't yer.

(The door bell rings.)

COSTELLO: *(Distort.)* Ruairi?

RUAIRI: The Big Fellah. Make yersen decent Michael. How do you work this?

(MICHAEL goes to his room. RUAIRI eventually works it out, and buzzes COSTELLO in.)

KARELMA: Who is this guy?

RUAIRI: You'll have to be on your way down the road now lover. And don't you go worrying about hurting me feelings last night. I been punched every day of me fucking life.

(Enter COSTELLO carrying a briefcase.)

COSTELLO: Is this it?

RUAIRI: Yeah.

(COSTELLO takes a walk around the flat getting a feel of the dimensions. He opens the bathroom door, looks in. He stops, as if shocked, under the guitar on the wall.)

RUAIRI: I know.

(Enter MICHAEL, dressed.)

COSTELLO: Michael?

MICHAEL: Yes sir.

COSTELLO: OK.

(To KARELMA.) Goodbye honey.

KARELMA: Heeeey, man

MICHAEL: Karelma it looks like –

KARELMA: – no way man. I'm your guest. Stand up to them Doyle.

MICHAEL: This has been a long standing arrangement. That we would bring the buckets back here, and Mr. Costello would collect them.

KARELMA: OK. Collect the motherfucking buckets.

MICHAEL: *(To COSTELLO.)* I'm sorry. *(To KARELMA.)* It's been nice to meet you.

KARELMA: I'm not leaving. You'll have to get these IRA boys to shoot me.

(Mr. COSTELLO looks at RUAIRI.)

I'm staying man.

(Mr. COSTELLO sits and opens his briefcase on the coffee table. He takes out a revolver and places it on the top of the case. KARELMA stands, quickly, and then exits to the spare room. MICHAEL follows her there.)

KARELMA: *(Off.)* Get out!

(*Michael is pushed out of the room.*)

MICHAEL: Karelma –

KARELMA: – fuck you Doyle.

(*KARELMA walks straight past MICHAEL and out. MICHAEL follows her into the lobby area.*)

MICHAEL: – wait!

(*COSTELLO stands by the door, and inspects the lock casually. He then closes the door, effectively locking MICHAEL out.*)

RUAIRI: Work quite well, eh, as a little safe house I mean.

COSTELLO: Yeah.

RUAIRI: He's got the three rooms back there, so one for himself, that's two for us. Is it to be Canada? For me? Do you know yet?

COSTELLO: I wanna talk to you about that.

(*MICHAEL knocks. COSTELLO lets him in.*)

Michael, would you mind, I need to have a word with Ruairi in private. I like the apartment. It's kinda …perfect.

MICHAEL: OK sir, I'll er…OK.

(*MICHAEL goes into his room.*)

RUAIRI: I wished you hadn't busted me out if it's gonna be Canada, I was doing well in the prison art class.

COSTELLO: It was Canada. But I got a call this morning. Orders. They want you to stay in New York.

RUAIRI: That's insane! It's only a matter of time before the FBI haul me up.

(*COSTELLO stands. With his thumb indicates MICHAEL's room.*)

COSTELLO: Is this guy serious?

RUAIRI: Yeah. I've been very rigorous with him. He's a big butty of Tom Billy, and his family are Galway people, you know, way back.

COSTELLO: For a RA boy like you, what's the easiest guy to kill?

RUAIRI: A Brit soldier? No. A stickie? No, a tout. Yeah, a tout.

COSTELLO: A tout. Could Michael kill a tout?

RUAIRI: No. He's a fireman. He saves lives. Sorry. I'll tell him it's a no.

COSTELLO: Wait. Do you play chess?

RUAIRI: I've not played since the Kesh.

COSTELLO: What's the most powerful piece on the board?

RUARI: The King. No. The Queen?

COSTELLO: The pawns. They don't run around whacking people, but there's a lot of them, and if you hang on to them, they're always there, quietly –

RUAIRI: – ah! he's quiet enough alright!

COSTELLO: – supporting us, the glory boys. I like him.

(COSTELLO opens MICHAEL's door. We see MICHAEL sitting passively on his bed drinking coffee.)

COSTELLO: I changed my mind.

MICHAEL: OK.

(MICHAEL comes out and sits slightly at a tangent to the COSTELLO / RUAIRI conversation. The following is now a performance from COSTELLO.)

COSTELLO: History is not made by men who take the easy road.

RUAIRI: Oh fuck. Listen, I'm a foot soldier, you and your big men can have the history books.

COSTELLO: You killed a British soldier in an ambush –

RUAIRI: – I didn't shoot him, I was only the driver.

COSTELLO: What did you put on your immigration form at JFK?

RUAIRI: I was on a forged passport, so it was hardly me own fucking immigration form now was it. Architect.

COSTELLO: And the box where it asks you "Have you any previous criminal convictions?" I imagine, since you're sitting here on Manhattan Island six months later you musta checked "none", "no criminal convictions"?

RUAIRI: Yeah.

COSTELLO: OK. The orders from Dublin are that you turn yourself in –

(RUAIRI stands.)

RUAIRI: – no fucking way!

COSTELLO: – And invite an American court, to decide whether an Irishman who kills a British soldier is politically motivated, or a criminal. D'yer get it?

MICHAEL: It's brilliant.

RUAIRI: Yeah well you haven't just spent two years in a fucking Brit jail.

MICHAEL: Yeah, but a New York jury gonna find for you man.

COSTELLO: One month after Bloody Sunday. The clever money's on you.

RUAIRI: Yeah, well I was a jockey and I've lost count of the number of times the favourite's broke a leg at the first fence and got shot by the veterinary.

COSTELLO: My attorney will represent you. And the mayor will name a street in your honour.

MICHAEL: Hey man! Fifth avenue becomes O'Drisceoil Way!

RUAIRI: And would they chuck in a visa? I'm serious about the architecture.

COSTELLO: How are you for money?

RUAIRI: I'm down to the bones of me bum.

(COSTELLO takes out a roll and gives it to RUAIRI.)

RUAIRI: These are orders yeah?

COSTELLO: Yeah. You got coffee here Michael?

MICHAEL: Sure thing.

(MICHAEL gets up and goes to the kitchen area and starts making a new pot of coffee for the Bialetti machine leaving RUAIRI and COSTELLO in what is essentially a two hander.)

COSTELLO: I didn't know you were a jockey.

RUAIRI: Yeah, do you like the horses yourself?

COSTELLO: It's my passion.

RUAIRI: Yeah. Cos when I was inside I come up with this idea for fund raising. I've done a bit of research and over here the best horse for me idea would be Captain Pickles. Have you heard of a horse called Captain Pickles?

COSTELLO: Yeah.

RUAIRI: Captain Pickles is retired and worth six million at stud. The boys steal him away, hide him up somewheres and ask for a ransom. The beauty of kidnaping a horse is they're not that bothered about escaping, and –

COSTELLO: – horses can't talk.

RUAIRI: Exactly!

COSTELLO: Except Mr. Ed.

RUAIRI: Jesus! That's not a bad idea. A talking horse must be worth a fucking fortune, and you've still got the inherent advantage, even with Mr. Ed, that it can't talk.

COSTELLO: Do you know who owns Captain Pickles?

RUAIRI: It'll be one of them Arabs, which is perfect, cos they don't know the value of money. Have you ever seen Captain Pickles race?

COSTELLO: Yes. Thirty three times.

RUAIRI: Fucking hell! That's his whole career.

COSTELLO: I've seen all of his races Ruairi.

RUAIRI: Ha! You must be his number one fucking fan!

COSTELLO: I am.

RUAIRI: Do you own any horses yourself Mr. Costello?

COSTELLO: Just the one.

RUAIRI: We'll pick a different horse.

(MICHAEL delivers coffees to the table. Mugs, and a carton of milk. All a bit blokey.)

COSTELLO: This is the kinda place we need Michael. I guess ya realise that looking after a safe house for us, cannot be separated from becoming one of us?

MICHAEL: Sure.

COSTELLO: We have people every year come through New York. Guys on the run like Ruairi, engineers buying stuff. They kick their heels for a month before we get them into Canada.

RUAIRI: *(Tapping the side of his nose.)* Unless we get orders to send them to Mexico.

MICHAEL: Do we have people in Mexico?

COSTELLO: *(Looking at RUAIRI.)* We have absolutely no connections with Mexico Michael.

(COSTELLO takes out a note book and pen.)

COSTELLO: OK. Is there any history of mental illness in your family?

MICHAEL: No.

COSTELLO: You got a girlfriend?

MICHAEL: No.

RUAIRI: He's awful laconic. He likes his little "nos", and that does it for him.

COSTELLO: Are you a homosexual?

MICHAEL: No.

(Beat. COSTELLO writes something down. It looks like he's moved on from homosexuality.)

COSTELLO: How do you know you're not a homosexual?

MICHAEL: I have feelings for women.

(COSTELLO writes something down.)

COSTELLO: Are you a communist?

MICHAEL: No.

COSTELLO: Vegetarian?

MICHAEL: No.

(COSTELLO writes something down. He then closes the book and puts it and his pen away.)

COSTELLO: This will seriously fuck your life. There is hardly a woman out there who would marry into the IRA.

MICHAEL: I understand.

COSTELLO: Do you know the story of Faust and the devil?

MICHAEL: No.

COSTELLO: This guy Faust sells his soul to the devil in exchange for twenty years of glory. What you're doing here, son, is Faust in reverse. Selling your soul for a lifetime of pain.

MICHAEL: I understand…yeah…it will make life more difficult, I guess.

COSTELLO: It will fuck your life. Tell me, how will it fuck your life?

MICHAEL: You know, like, er…finding a woman who would knowingly marry into the IRA.

RUAIRI: – 'cept Elizabeth Ryan herself.

COSTELLO: Ruairi.

RUAIRI: She's single. A lot of the boys have had a crack at her I know that, but none of them got nowhere. She's a lot sharper than that gobshite Danny Morrision and shoulda got Head of Publicity instead of him. Yeah she's definitely one of the intellectuals I would say, and possibly the first President of All Ireland Don't you think Mr. Costello? Imagine that, and a woman an'all.

(COSTELLO glares at him.)

I'll shut up now.

COSTELLO: I only have the one child, Graunia. She's eleven. Every year we take her to the parade. For the first time last night she came to the dinner. We get home, she asks me "Daddy, what's the money for?". You're not just fucking up your own life. Those you love, they godda clear choice, they don't love you no more, or they're in deep with you. So tell me again. What will this mean for your life?

MICHAEL: It will fuck my life.

COSTELLO: Well done Michael. Looking good.

(They laugh.)

COSTELLO: You look at me and you see this coat, this watch, the shoes – outside a new Lincoln Cadillac. They call me the Big Fellah. Bullshit. It's an army. I'm a soldier. I get orders. I fucking jump. I'm a dumbass like every other dumbass. A lot of the time I'm doing shit I don't wanna do.

MICHAEL: I understand.

COSTELLO: Loose talk. There was a guy we had. One time, with a woman, I guess he was tryna screw her, he told her he was a freedom fighter in the IRA.

RUAIRI: Gillespie? I never met him but me brother said he had a tongue on him. Did he get fucking Mexicoed?!

COSTELLO: Do you need a dump?

RUAIRI: Sorry.

MICHAEL: I think I understand Mexico.

(MICHAEL puts mimes a gun to the head and a shot.)

COSTELLO: I guess what happened in Derry got you angry? I celebrated.

MICHAEL: I guess the more we're attacked, the stronger we become.

COSTELLO: Exactly.

RUAIRI: Ah, Jesus. I'll never be a fucking officer.

(COSTELLO takes out an envelope from his briefcase and gives it to MICHAEL.)

COSTELLO: You will attend a weekend upstate. At the end of that period you will be assessed again, and if both parties are happy, you will be sworn in. Now Ruairi has briefed me on your background, and motivation, but is there anything I need to know about you before we start this whole process?

MICHAEL: One thing. My family, my Irish family, my ancestors, if you like, and I guess me now too, er…strictly speaking, what I'm trying to say is – I'm a Protestant.

(After a period of silence during which RUAIRI looks at the floor, and rubs his head and COSTELLO seems unmoved, RUAIRI stands and goes to the kitchen, and fiddles clumsily with the coffee pot.)

COSTELLO: Ruairi?

RUAIRI: Sorry, look I –

COSTELLO: – Name the greatest Irishman.

RUAIRI: Er… Michael Collins? No? William Butler Yeats. No. Johnny Giles? Er…fuck. What was the name of that other fucking play writer fellah?

COSTELLO: Who was the father of Irish Nationalism?

RUAIRI: Oh, I didn't know you were going that far back. Wolfe Tone, o' course.

COSTELLO: Wolfe Tone described British rule over Ireland as a disease. He raised an army in France and sailed to Ireland. The Irish farmers joined his army in battle. Men, women, and children armed with sticks faced the English canon. They were slaughtered. Wolfe Tone was sentenced to death. In his cell he cut his own throat with a pen knife. I've stood on his grave Michael. Bodenstown, County Kildare. And what I sense when I stand there in that tumbledown cemetery is that I am standing on the holiest sod of all Ireland, holier even than the place where Patrick sleeps in Down. Wolfe Tone was a Protestant.

RUAIRI: Beautiful.

COSTELLO: OK. Let's count this fucking money.

(They begin sorting money and stuffing wads into the holdall.)

End of scene

Act 2

SCENE 1

(1981. An art gallery. A couple of paintings, both Mondrians. RUAIRI is looking at them. He is impressed. Enter KARELMA in business work clothes, new hair do.)

KARELMA: Ruairi? You remember me.

RUAIRI: I think I do but –

KARELMA: – different outfit.

RUAIRI: Yes, now, no, bollocks. Michael's place. Jesus, Mary and the fucking donkey! Did we?

KARELMA: No. We didn't.

RUAIRI: Bloody Sunday.

KARELMA: Nine years.

RUAIRI: What is this? Black businesswoman of the year awards. I forgotten yer name, so I have!

MICHAEL: Karelma.

RUAIRI: Are yer running for President!?

KARELMA: I'm working in Wall Street, just two blocks, you know –

RUAIRI: – Well fuck me! You got yerself legal then?

KARELMA: Yeah.

RUAIRI: And you won't be rolling no spliffs, or sleeping with the likes of me then?

KARELMA: No.

RUAIRI: Not that you did that afore like.

KARELMA: I've been following your court case –

RUAIRI: – ah, yer a fan now are yer?

KARELMA: It's been running longer than the Mary Tyler Moore show.

RUAIRI: Yeah, I hope to win a fucking whatyercallit –

KARELMA: – an Emmi.

RUAIRI: – aye, an Emmi award would be nice before I get slammed up.

KARELMA: I'm so proud of you. And – the other day I met a friend on "O'Drisceoil corner".

RUAIRI: They said it was gonna be a whole street.

KARELMA: Having a corner is much better than a street For going anywhere around 53rd and 3rd people say meet you on O'Drisceoil corner.

RUAIRI: Yeah. I'm famous.

KARELMA: Do you like Mondrian then?

RUAIRI: Aye, and there's always a lot of single women in an art gallery, it's like shooting fish in a barrel. But anywhere that's licenced and don't play Irish music is fine by me.

KARELMA: You don't like Irish music?

RUAIRI: It's the soundtrack of hell.

KARELMA: D'you wanna sit, I've got a minute?

RUAIRI: Sure.

(They sit on a viewing bench.)

Look at yer! You buying and selling the world then?

KARELMA: I'm a journalist. Hey, look I, we do a monthly investment bulletin on Europe, ya know, updated monthly, yeah, and I got the Irish desk, wow! Maybe I could interview you sometime. Cos everyone knows you, and what you have is that smack of truth, yeah? This month I have to do a thousand words on County Wicklow.

RUAIRI: I know fuck all about Wicklow.

KARELMA: No, no, it's about how the Irish think, like, I want to do something on what the Irish feel about the attempted assassination of Ronald Reagan.

RUAIRI: What – cos Reagan thinks he's Irish you mean?

KARELMA: Do Irish Americans think of Reagan as Irish?

RUAIRI: They know he's Irish, but they don't love him like they love the Irish who've done well for themselves over here – like JFK or Billy the Kid.

KARELMA: But do the Irish in Ireland think Reagan is Irish?

RUAIRI: They think he's an eijit someone built for a laugh.

KARELMA: That's real funny man. Look, I can afford a hundred dollars a month. You know, if we could do just one interview a month, maybe an hour.

RUAIRI: I talk bullshit for an hour and then you give me a hundred dollars?

KARELMA: You got it.

RUAIRI: I've been talking bollocks as an amateur for years, I'm not sure I'm ready to step up to professional.

KARELMA: Think about it. I'll need an IRS invoice.

RUAIRI: I'm not an American.

KARELMA: You've not got a visa?

RUAIRI: A visa is exactly what I've not got.

KARELMA: But I thought with the bail bond you got –

RUAIRI: – killing a British soldier –

KARELMA: – which you didn't do man, you were the driver.

RUAIRI: – aye, but you'll remember they dug up me long history of house breaking which even Henry Fonda himself couldn't stretch to calling a political act.

KARELMA: A lawyer friend of mine works for the Donnelly commission. Her whole life is looking at naturalisation cases like yours. D'you wanna meet?

RUAIRI: If she can fix it, yeah.

KARELMA: Here's my card. Give me a call tomorrow.

RUAIRI: Are you an angel? This has been the greatest day of me life so far.

End of scene.

SCENE 2

(September 14th 1981. Music plays – Roxy Music's "If it takes all night" from the album Country Life – on vinyl. The apartment much the same, but with the odd improvement, including a Manchester United scarf. MICHAEL's FDNY coat with logo is thrown on the floor, as are other clothes. MICHAEL, with pants round his ankles and T shirt pushed up to his chin, lies in the arms of ELIZABETH. ELIZABETH is a 30ish Irish woman. She's attractive, but what dominates in her face is her wit and intelligence. As we open they are breathy, and recovering. The Roxy Music track plays out, and the LP ends and the arm of the player cranks off.)

ELIZABETH: You were saying. Earlier.

MICHAEL: – earlier?

ELIZABETH: Before we got involved in all this.

MICHAEL: What?

ELIZABETH: You were boring the pants off me with tales of your younger self abroad in Peru. A mural in a restaurant?

MICHAEL: OK, yeah, the mural. Right, so there's Jesus Christ, yeah?

ELIZABETH: What do you mean? "Jesus Christ, yeah"
    – question mark? Are you insulting me Michael?

MICHAEL: I don't get –

ELIZABETH: – Are you seriously checking to see if I know who
    Jesus Christ is?

MICHAEL: No.

ELIZABETH: I presume you're talking about the Son of God
    Jesus Christ, or did you mean Jesus Christ the well known
    Peruvian short order chef?

MICHAEL: I'm sorry.

ELIZABETH: You're in a restaurant in Peru with Tom Billy
    Coyle and there's this massive mural on the wall which is
    obviously –

MICHAEL: – they're eating a meal.

ELIZABETH: – the last supper.

MICHAEL: How did you know that?

ELIZABETH: It was the menu I guess. As in "To start I'll have a
    Saint Thomas, and then a main course Judas Escariat".

MICHAEL: Yeah, you're right. But you'll never guess what
    Jesus is eating?

ELIZABETH: Guinea pig.

MICHAEL: How did you know that?

ELIZABETH: Everyone knows that they eat guinea pig in Peru.
    And there wouldn't be a story unless it was Jesus Christ
    himself eating the fucking guinea pig.

MICHAEL: Am I dumb?

ELIZABETH: Oh Michael.

(She kisses him.)

You're pretty good at some things.

MICHAEL: Did you come?

ELIZABETH: No. All that wailing and thrashing me arm about was me faking it.

(MICHAEL starts to move himself off.)

Where are you going?

MICHAEL: Ruairi should be back by now and the Big Fellah's got his own keys, and, you know, look at us.

ELIZABETH: Kiss me.

(MICHAEL kisses her.)

MICHAEL: Oh God I love you.

ELIZABETH: I'm trying not to slip into the love thing with you but with my knickers around my ankles, and my bra round my neck I surely must be losing.

(They kiss.)

MICHAEL: They might want you to go to Canada.

ELIZABETH: That is why it's important we don't do the love thing.

MICHAEL: Let's get married.

ELIZABETH: No fucking way. Marriage is the institutionalised oppression of women, and brings on a capitulation to sameness.

MICHAEL: What does that mean?

ELIZABETH: After a month we'd be wearing matching anoraks.

(They kiss again, a deep sensual kiss.)

MICHAEL: I don't understand why it's me.

ELIZABETH: You, yer stuck out, like a beautiful sore thumb. When you came round the corner at the funeral, heading

up that bunch of phonies you got the nerve to call a pipe
band

MICHAEL: – the award winning New York Hibernia Society
Police Band.

ELIZABETH: It was comical, but there was something
compelling about you, you I mean, Michael. Some kind
of innocence. I might even be here to save yer soul, who
knows.

MICHAEL: For me…when you walked out of the Ard Fheis
that time, just, you know, you shouted something to the
leadership, all those men, I don't remember what you said,
but I watched your face, and their faces, and you walked
out and they were scared. And I don't know what it was
you'd said but I knew that they knew you were right.

ELIZABETH: "Welcome to the misogyny club AGM!"

MICHAEL: Yeah, that was it. What's a misogynist? Is that like –

ELIZABETH: – a sexist, anti-women.

MICHAEL: I worked it out.

ELIZABETH: We don't mention "us" to the Big Fellah. OK.

MICHAEL: Ruairi will have blagged us already, you can put
your life on that.

ELIZABETH: Aye, I guess. I doubt the Big Fellah's got any
influence over the decision.

MICHAEL: If it's Canada – .

ELIZABETH: – don't! We don't know where I've got to go
lover. We can't make plans.

*(ELIZABETH stands and goes through to the bedroom. MICHAEL
dresses and continues to talk.)*

MICHAEL: I'll just walk outa the firehouse. I could do it. I can
find work in Toronto.

(Re-enter ELIZABETH wearing a dressing gown.)

ELIZABETH: You won't. I won't let you. You can visit if it's Canada, but it might be Libya, and I don't care how much you love me I can't see you popping over to Tripoli for a fuck every other weekend.

MICHAEL: We don't have anyone in Libya.

ELIZABETH: After me court martial O'Neill said, after he said I was fucking lucky to be alive, he said Libya had become a posting.

MICHAEL: Why did he say you were lucky to be alive?

ELIZABETH: The court martial wasn't unanimous.

MICHAEL: But you were told to set the guy up!

ELIZABETH: I'd been seeing a Brit for two years. That was enough for some of them.

MICHAEL: But it wouldna been two years if Belfast had hit the guy when they shoulda hit the guy.

ELIZABETH: But they didn't.

MICHAEL: Why didn't they?

ELIZABETH: I dunno.

MICHAEL: Did you fall in love with him, the Brit?

ELIZABETH: Frig no! I was sick of the fucking oik. The truth is Michael I was a threat to Belfast, they didn't like me, they hate women you see –

MICHAEL: – misogyny!

ELIZABETH: *(Nod to MICHAEL.)* – so they let me go with the Brit for long enough to make it look like a fucking relationship, which made me look like a tout. That's the top and bottom of it. They didn't want a woman in the leadership.

MICHAEL: Why didn't Dublin hit the guy?

ELIZABETH: I was in Belfast. It's tribal.

(There is a buzzer at the door.)

We'll find out now. Canada. Please God!

MICHAEL: Canada.

ELIZABETH: I'm in the shower.

(ELIZABETH gives him a final peck, and goes into the bathroom. MICHAEL attends to the intercom.)

COSTELLO: *(Distort.)* It's me.

(MICHAEL buzzes him in. He gets himself a beer. Hides one of her socks in his pocket. COSTELLO enters, very drunk. He tries the bathroom door which, to his disgust, he finds is locked.)

COSTELLO: I need a piss.

MICHAEL: Miss Ryan is in the shower.

COSTELLO: I'll piss in the sink.

MICHAEL: Please, sir, no.

COSTELLO: Have you got a bucket?

MICHAEL: No.

COSTELLO: Ten years ago, you had eighteen fucking buckets. How's it been? With her staying here. Huh?

MICHAEL: Like all the others.

COSTELLO: All the others were guys.

MICHAEL: Nothing sir. I swear. We haven't even…nothing.

COSTELLO: It's not Libya.

MICHAEL: No?

(COSTELLO stands underneath the guitar.)

COSTELLO: If Frank McArdle ever sees this – he'll kill you. He's very big on traditional Irish music. Frank once killed a guy with a spade for wearing a shirt and tie set, in mustard. Have you got whiskey?

MICHAEL: Did you drive here Mr. Costello?

COSTELLO: Tom Billy dropped me. He's outside.

MICHAEL: He can come in. We got food enough. Ruairi's picking up a Chinese to go.

COSTELLO: No. I want him out there.

MICHAEL: It's not Libya then. Good.

COSTELLO: Why do you care Michael?

(Enter ELIZABETH in bathrobe.)

ELIZABETH: Mister Costello, good to see you. We've met once before. Bodenstown. The cemetery.

COSTELLO: I don't remember.

(COSTELLO goes into the bathroom for a piss. He starts pissing with the door open. MICHAEL has to close the door behind him.)

ELIZABETH: He's as pissed as a fart. Did he say anything?

MICHAEL: It's not Libya.

(ELIZABETH goes into the spare room. MICHAEL tidies up some more. MICHAEL goes to get a drink, sits, feels that something is wrong. He looks out of the window. COSTELLO comes out of the bathroom. Enter ELIZABETH. She is now dressed.)

COSTELLO: What do you do two?

ELIZABETH: What do "we do two"?

COSTELLO: No. What do you two do? I've been drinking. What do you do two when he's not putting fucking fires out?

ELIZABETH: I've not sat around wasting time Mr. Costello. I wrote that article on the hunger strikers or have you not read it? And I've been waiting for an invitation from you for me to speak to the Hibernia Society about Bobby, and funding for a statue.

COSTELLO: When I came back from Korea, I didn't have Jack shit. I spent my vet's grant on a Chrysler. Then I got another Chrysler. I was living off two Chryslers. It's possible. And a wife. But every day, every day that God sent, a clean shirt. Fucking K Mart shirt – yeah! and twenty dollar suit yeah! but clean. I'll tell you what I didn't do! I didn't walk around with my hair down to my ass. I didn't cake the walls of my car rental cabin with my own excrement! MY WAR is not a whinge against capitalism. What do they say they want?

ELIZABETH: A democratic socialist republic.

COSTELLO: Yeah, fucking communists!

(Enter RUAIRI with Chinese meal. RUAIRI goes straight to sit down at the coffee table.)

RUAIRI: I'm starving! I could eat the holy lamb outa God's right hand and fuck the consequences. Are yer alright there Mr. Costello?

COSTELLO: Ruairi! Question!

RUAIRI: Ah fuck! I've just walked in the door!

COSTELLO: Tell this boy here why Frank McArdle killed Bernie Toolis with a spade. It was the mustard shirt and tie set wasn't it!

RUAIRI: It weren't mustard, it was peach.

(COSTELLO stands.)

COSTELLO: It was fucking mustard!

(RUAIRI stands, mocking him.)

RUAIRI: It was fucking peachy, apricoty, salmony thing!

MICHAEL: Did it have a pattern or was it plain?

RUAIRI: Plain, it was completely unrelenting! The odd stripe or check or galloping horse woulda helped us all. The only sense of detail it had was the fucking epaulettes. Also in peach.

COSTELLO: Mustard!

ELIZABETH: Frank didn't kill Bernie cos of that shirt.

COSTELLO: Are you implying that I don't know the history of my nation's struggle?

ELIZABETH: Bernie died cos he accused Frank of raping his brother in law in the Maze. The shirt and tie thing was neither here nor there. So, my advice about Frank McArdle is "wear what the fuck you like but don't ever suggest that he's a violent rapist".

(COSTELLO sits. He's lost the argument and given up.)

RUAIRI: *(To COSTELLO.)* You'd do well to write that down.

ELIZABETH: I hate Frank McArdle with a loathing that I cannot describe but if we didn't have him, we'd have to invent him. I'm talking about the role and function of oral history, and myth making in keeping up the morale of an underequipped people's volunteer army. *(Beat.)* And I'm being a bit ironic too.

MICHAEL: We've had a month o' that kind of chat. Do you want to eat with us Mr. Costello?

COSTELLO: I've eaten!

RUAIRI: And yer been on the juice an'all!

(COSTELLO stands.)

COSTELLO: Who Ruairi!? –

RUAIRI: – Ah fuck.

COSTELLO: – Who is the beating heart of the IRA?

RUAIRI: Every time wid you yer giving me a fresh round in the quiz of life. I'll guess you mean the Catholic, or the Nationalist.

COSTELLO: The farmer!

RUAIRI: I was gonna say the cow farmer but the way yer put it made the question sound more difficult than it was.

COSTELLO: It's not these Belfast hippies.

ELIZABETH: Concur. Belfast has got too much influence now.

COSTELLO: My daughter, she went to Brown University. It took them two months, two fucking months –

RUAIRI: – come on let's eat. Miss Ryan doesn't need to know none of this.

ELIZABETH: It took who two months to do what – to your daughter?

RUAIRI: That's your plate there.

COSTELLO: Narcotics.

RUAIRI: We've all done drugs, it's all part of growing up nowadays and –

COSTELLO: – Now, she's a junkie.

RUAIRI: Na, she's young and having a bit of a laugh.

COSTELLO: My little girl.

RUAIRI: Just a phase.

COSTELLO: And these Belfast long hairs, they wanna nationalise the land! Ha! Hypothetical choice! You can have a united Ireland, BUT yer have to give the family farm to Gerry Adams!

RUAIRI: *(Laughs.)*

COSTELLO: OR! You can keep your land, but three times a day you have to salute the Queen of England! Ruairi! What would happen?!

RUAIRI: There'd be a portrait of Elizabeth the Second on every fucking fridge!

COSTELLO: Thank you! Bobby Sands! Carried my bag. Polite. He will go down in Irish history, but the others. Who gives a fuck about who dies sixth, or seventh?! I bet you none of you can name any single one of the others.

ELIZABETH: Francis Hughes, Raymond McCreesh, Patsy O'Hara, Joe McDonnell, Martin Hurson, Kevin Lynch, Kieran Doherty, Thomas McElwee, and Michael Devine.

RUAIRI: Ha, ha, that's shut you up.

(COSTELLO sits.)

COSTELLO: *(To ELIZABETH, as if the others know.)* In this town the firemen, the cops, they spend all day busting longhairs, if this goes on they're gonna stop giving money for the war. Cops don't give money to hippies. You know how much money we took after Bloody Sunday?

MICHAEL: – six hundred thousand dollars.

COSTELLO: – this year!?

MICHAEL: Less than a hundred thousand.

COSTELLO: We need money to keep this fucking celebrity going with his TV appearances and his attorney's champagne breakfasts. Ha!

(Slaps RUAIRI on the back.)

All around the world Ruairi is known as a martyr.

RUAIRI: Except Downing Street where the phrase they use is "murdering bastard".

MICHAEL: You were only the driver.

ELIZABETH: Can you not get Ruairi a visa Mr. Costello. He wants to be an architect.

COSTELLO: He was a certified felon before he was a –

RUAIRI: – Prisoner of Conscience. I got someone from the Donnelly commission working away at the visa. So God Bless America and who wants a crispy duck pancake?!

MICHAEL: Hit me.

ELIZABETH: Did you get my orders today? Do you know where they want me to go?

(Silence.)

Mister Costello?

COSTELLO: What is that?

MICHAEL: Squid!

COSTELLO: That's my favourite. Ruairi, can I ask you a question?

RUAIRI: For fuck's sake! Question three.

COSTELLO: This green book. Do you know why it's green?

RUAIRI: We're the IRA! We're not gonna have a fucking orange book are we!

COSTELLO: It's green for Islam.

RUAIRI: Yer drunk, and yer've had a tab of acid!

ELIZABETH: He's right. The "Green Book" is an homage to Qaddafi's terrorist manual.

RUAIRI: An "homage"? The IRA has been accused of many things lady, but one thing we're not is pretentious.

(COSTELLO stands knocking over his chair backwards.)

COSTELLO: What am I!? Ruairi!

RUAIRI: A squid lover. Now sit the fuck down!

COSTELLO: Am I a Muslim? Am I a communist!?

RUAIRI: No. I'll tell yer what yer are. Yer the very definition of the American dream. Yer started with fuck all and yer've ended up with too much.

COSTELLO: Am I a communist?

RUAIRI: We've done that one!

MICHAEL: For me, Mister Costello, you're a soldier. And you're an inspiration to me.

COSTELLO: Thank you son. Miss Ryan. What do you see?

ELIZABETH: I see a man usurped. A man who wanted to serve his country, to be remembered as a great Irishman, to do the right thing –

COSTELLO: – to go down in history!

ELIZABETH: But his country looked to someone new. I see a lover, rejected.

(Silence.)

RUAIRI: Ah fuck. This is me only night off yer know!

COSTELLO: She's right! Go on.

ELIZABETH: Ten years ago you gave us the Armalite Rifle. I stood next to you in the cemetery at Bodenstown.

COSTELLO: The respect!

ELIZABETH: I was nineteen. Shoulder to shoulder with a hero in the rain.

RUAIRI: Ah! Now was it raining?! Well fuck me!

ELIZABETH: Somebody pointed you out. "That fellah, there, the big fellah, he's the American".

COSTELLO: The American. That's what they called me!

ELIZABETH: Where did you get those rifles Mr. Costello?

COSTELLO: In America there's two main sources of guns. The Italians.

ELIZABETH: The Mafia?

RUAIRI: Aye.

ELIZABETH: And what's the second source?

COSTELLO: The shops.

(They all laugh. RUAIRI takes a mouthful.)

RUAIRI: Fucking hell that's hot. What is that?

MICHAEL: Shredded beef in chilli.

RUAIRI: Give me another beer. Quick!

(MICHAEL obliges.)

ELIZABETH: But we don't count the rifles we get from Qaddafi. We weigh them in tons.

COSTELLO: And what is Qaddafi buying? Our motherfucking souls! We're all international socialists now!

(COSTELLO sits.)

RUAIRI: Yer finished now are yer?

ELIZABETH: Mr. Costello. You're staring at me.

RUAIRI: Elizabeth says that the Army Council are keen on me horse napping idea. Taking it very seriously and looking for a big Irish horse.

ELIZABETH: It's a great idea.

(COSTELLO goes to the window and gestures to TOM BILLY.)

RUAIRI: What yer doing? Who you got out there?

MICHAEL: Tom Billy.

RUAIRI: And what's the fat fuck sitting out there for?

COSTELLO: I feel sick.

RUAIRI: Ah fuck, that's all we need.

(MICHAEL stands and helps COSTELLO into the bathroom, where he leaves him. The sound of vomiting. Loud and long.)

RUAIRI: *(Pushing his plate away.)* That's done it for me.

(MICHAEL starts clearing the food and plates away. The intercom buzzes. MICHAEL goes to it.)

TOM BILLY: *(Distort.)* Tom Billy.

(MICHAEL buzzes him in.)

RUAIRI: Costello must know where yer going or he wouldn't come round.

ELIZABETH: That's why he said he was coming round.

(Enter TOM BILLY, silent, serious looking.)

TOM BILLY: Where's the Big Fellah?

RUAIRI: He's in there painting the carpet.

(COSTELLO comes out of the bathroom. He looks steadier.)

COSTELLO: You're here.

TOM BILLY: Yeah. I'm here.

COSTELLO: Miss Ryan! Get your things. We've got orders.

ELIZABETH: I'm not going anywhere.

COSTELLO: Ruairi! Go and get her things.

RUAIRI: Ah fuck, I've just got me feet under the table.

COSTELLO: She's going. She has to go tonight.

TOM BILLY: It's a long drive. We gotta go now.

(RUAIRI stands.)

ELIZABETH: Where am I going?

COSTELLO: Mexico.

ELIZABETH: Mexico? By car?

MICHAEL: No, not Mexico. Mister Costello –

COSTELLO: Be quiet Michael!

(MICHAEL stands.)

Sit down.

(MICHAEL remains standing.)

ELIZABETH: What's going on?

COSTELLO: These are orders. Sit down.

TOM BILLY: Sit down Michael.

(MICHAEL sits.)

ELIZABETH: Where exactly in Mexico am I going?

COSTELLO: Acapulco.

MICHAEL: No. No! NO!

(MICHAEL stands, now desperate.)

COSTELLO: Michael! Get in your room! I'm telling you – get in your room and shut the door. That's also an order.

TOM BILLY: These are all fucking orders!

ELIZABETH: Michael! What's happening?

COSTELLO: Keep the noise down!

(To MICHAEL.) Get in that room.

(To ELIZABETH.) You, get your coat.

COSTELLO: Michael! Go to your room.

TOM BILLY: Buddy, I think it's best if you go to your fucking room now! This is an operation.

MICHAEL: No!

(TOM BILLY goes over to MICHAEL and takes his arm. MICHAEL is crying and moaning.)

TOM BILLY: Come on Michael. Now, quit the hollering. Get up!

(MICHAEL gets up.)

ELIZABETH: Whose orders are these? Is it Army Council?

COSTELLO: Put your coat on lady.

(MICHAEL submits and is led to his room by TOM BILLY. TOM BILLY closes the door.)

TOM BILLY: Ruairi. Here.

(TOM BILLY posts RUAIRI on guard outside MICHAEL's room.)

RUAIRI: Ah, fuck.

ELIZABETH: Michael, help me!

(MICHAEL opens the door.)

COSTELLO: Keep that fucking door closed!

(RUAIRI slams the door shut. COSTELLO vomits into the sink.)

TOM BILLY: Take it easy sir. If you wanna help lady, put yer coat on.

ELIZABETH: No. I'm not going anywhere. We have no operation in Mexico. I demand to see the orders.

TOM BILLY: You're a tout lady.

COSTELLO: *(To TOM BILLY.)* That's enough.

ELIZABETH: I was exonerated at my court martial. You know that.

TOM BILLY: You know what happens to touts.

ELIZABETH: Michael! They're gonna kill me!

COSTELLO: Ruairi, put some fucking music on!

(During the next RUAIRI goes over the record player and sticks the needle on the album which is on the turntable. It's side one of Roxy Music's Country Life album. RUAIRI clumsily sticks the needle on the first track "The Thrill of it All". He turns the volume up.)

ELIZABETH: Michael! Michael!! Help me!

TOM BILLY: Shut the fuck up!

(TOM BILLY goes into ELIZABETH's room and comes out with her coat, which he throws at her. She picks it up and throws it back at him. TOM BILLY draws his revolver and points it at her.)

ELIZABETH: Come on Michael! You can help me now! Michael! Break that door down!

(MICHAEL is barging the door and Ruairi struggles to keep it closed. ELIZABETH starts to snatch books from the shelves and throw them at TOM BILLY. MICHAEL eases the door open.)

COSTELLO: Keep outa this Michael! Get back in there!

ELIZABETH: Michael! Take the gun off him.

(COSTELLO brandishes his gun. MICHAEL backs off. The door is closed again.)

COSTELLO: Keep quiet. Keep calm.

(To RUAIRI.) Turn the music up!

(To TOM BILLY.) Knock her out!

(TOM BILLY approaches ELIZABETH. She throws books at him.)

ELIZABETH: Don't you fucking touch me!

COSTELLO: Knock her out!

(ELIZABETH and TOM BILLY wrestle. TOM BILLY eventually has her pinned to the floor where she screams.)

ELIZABETH: Michael! Help me! They're gonna kill me!

TOM BILLY: Give me the gun!

(TOM BILLY pistol whips her. She lies unconscious. COSTELLO turns the music off.)

COSTELLO: Right, let's go. Ruairi, give him a hand.

(RUAIRI lets the door go, and goes to help TOM BILLY. MICHAEL comes out and passively watches. TOM BILLY and RUAIRI are now out in the hall.)

NEIGHBOUR: *(Off.)* What's all the hollering man!?

TOM BILLY: *(Off.)* NYPD. Cut me some slack man! Just doing my job!

NEIGHBOUR: *(Off.)* OK, OK.

(COSTELLO stands in the doorway. MICHAEL doesn't know what to do with himself.)

MICHAEL: They gave you orders?

COSTELLO: I got orders.

MICHAEL: Shit man. What she do?

COSTELLO: We got orders.

(COSTELLO leaves. MICHAEL goes to the window and looks out. MICHAEL collapses on to his knees in the middle of the room, his head in his hands, weeping. RUAIRI comes back in and closes the door behind him. RUAIRI sits on the sofa. RUAIRI comforts MICHAEL.)

MICHAEL: *(Barely articulate.)* Ruairi, what's happened? What have they done?

RUAIRI: I like being in the IRA, but if there's one thing I'd change, it's all the fucking killing.

End of scene

INTERVAL .

Act 3

SCENE 1

(1987. The apartment. New furniture. The guitar is still there on the wall, but in a different place. It now seems symbolic, a combination of an act of defiance and a memorial to ELIZABETH. RUAIRI, dressed in a Hugo Boss suit, sits on the arm of the sofa. He has a can of Bud or similar open. Set downstage left is a tatty, cheap and old suit case and an old fashioned duffle bag. FRANK McARDLE sits in the centre of the three piece sofa, looking scary. He is dressed in shirt sleeves.)

FRANK: I shot the fucker.

RUAIRI: What?!

FRANK: Through the head. He died instantly.

RUAIRI: Yer shot Shergar!? How could yer shoot a beautiful horse like that?!

FRANK: He was going mad, kicking the fucking fuck out of the fucking horse box.

RUAIRI: Sure, did yer not think of trying him with a carrot first?

FRANK; I thought of that, aye, but it was already dark and all the shops were shut. Is that what you wear for work?

RUAIRI: I been at a clients. It's Hugo Boss. Do you, like it Frank?

FRANK: Makes you look like a cunt.

RUAIRI: Yeah.

FRANK: You got a good job then now?

RUAIRI: Architect.

FRANK: Fucking hell.

RUAIRI: I was born on a cow farm but I always knew that was not for me.

FRANK: What's wrong with cow farming?

RUAIRI: Nothing, nothing, no, no, no. We all godda eat, eh?

FRANK: You legal then?

RUAIRI: Yeah, been legal for six, seven year now, yeah. *(Beat.)* So Security thinks that it was one of us here in New York what betrayed that ship?

FRANK: Aye.

RUAIRI: A hundred and fifty tons of arms. Kaw! We coulda won the war in a week.

FRANK: How did you know it was a hundred and fifty tons?

RUAIRI: I read it in Time magazine.

FRANK: I godda have the other fellah here an'all.

RUAIRI: Doyle does his fireman's exams class thingy on a Tuesday, no! wait! it's band practice, aye. They let him play in the police pipe band for some reason and they're all going over to Donegal again to head up the Bobby Sands memorial march, aye.

FRANK: Are they any good?

RUAIRI: They sound like an abattoir with the doors open.

FRANK: Why are they letting them head up the march then?

RUAIRI: The Army Council are dead keen to have American law officers front up an IRA funeral, you know, it'll be on every world leader's telly

(RUAIRI taps the side of his nose knowingly.)

FRANK: – aye! that's clever. I need to see the Big Fellah himself.

RUAIRI: I told him to come along later, like yer said, aye, though you don't tell the Big Fellah what to do, understand. It mighta helped if yer'd told us you were coming Frank. And Tom Billy is on a shift, so yers'll have to see him tomorrow. *(Beat.)* And how is the lovely Mary?

FRANK: Aye.

RUAIRI: And yer eldest, the hairdresser? What's her name?

FRANK: Mary.

RUAIRI: Yeah.

FRANK: She married a strong farmer.

RUAIRI: That's a result. How many yer got left at home now?

FRANK: I got three of them married and three left at home.

RUAIRI: Six! Ha! That's a lot of daughters in any culture.

FRANK: Aye.

(RUAIRI lights up a cigarette.)

FRANK: Did I say you could fucking smoke?

RUAIRI: I'll get rid of the filthy thing.

(RUAIRI puts the cig out and bins it. He gets a beer from the fridge.)

(Beat.)

Am I alright with the beer?

FRANK: Aye.

RUAIRI: As a recovering alcoholic are you allowed the odd tin?

FRANK: Am I fuck.

RUAIRI: Do you go to Alcoholics Anonymous back there in Lurgan then?

FRANK: Aye.

RUAIRI: Is it a mixed group?

FRANK: Aye.

RUAIRI: Yer never think of Protestants as having a problem with the drink do yer. How do yer find the process? All that honesty, and publicly facing up to the empty sham of your existence? Has it affected yer fundamentally as a human being?

FRANK: Aye.

RUAIRI: In what way has it changed yer Frank?

FRANK: I've given up the drink.

RUAIRI: No?! Fucking hell! What do you do for fun?

FRANK: I fuck the wife.

RUAIRI: She'll be glad of the week off then.

FRANK: Aye. How do yous know you're not an alcoholic?

RUAIRI: Me? Na!

FRANK: Do you drink at home, alone, of an evening?

RUAIRI: Na, never! I'm always in the pub. So you're here for a week Frank?

FRANK: I might do the sights this time.

RUAIRI: There's a Kandinsky at the Museum of Modern Art? Fantastic! Russian fellah. Maybe a bit abstract for you.

FRANK: I like a good zoo.

RUAIRI: Yeah.

(FRANK stands and goes to look out the window, and during the next has a look around.)

FRANK: Tomorrow night could we go seek out some traditional Irish music?

RUAIRI: Ah, fuck.

FRANK: And I'm not going home until I've walked up and
down your street.

RUAIRI: You know that it's not a whole street, don't you? It's
like a corner.

FRANK: I don't care. I want to stand on O'Drisceoil corner.

RUAIRI: Aye, well, you might not want to when yer get there.

FRANK: How d'yer mean?

RUAIRI: It's become something of a spot for picking up rent
boys.

FRANK: What the fuck's a rent boy?

RUAIRI: Look, I know a good pub for Irish music only two
blocks down, will yer be happy with that?

FRANK: I like me music yer see.

(FRANK inspects the guitar on the wall.)

FRANK: Who the fuck did this? That's a musical instrument
that.

RUAIRI: Well it was aye.

(FRANK sits.)

RUAIRI: The Big Fellah's all sore about the whole family thing,
and I'd best avoid it as a topic of conversation if I were
you.

FRANK: I'm Security, I can ask any questions that take me
fancy.

RUAIRI: All I'm saying, for the sake of everyone, if you keep
off the subject of his daughter. And the wife.

FRANK: Theresa. She gone?

RUAIRI: Yeah.

(Enter MICHAEL in kilt with bagpipes.)

RUAIRI: This is –

FRANK: – did you do that?

MICHAEL: Yes.

(FRANK punches MICHAEL in the stomach. MICHAEL collapses on the floor. FRANK empties his duffle bag on to the sofa, slips the duffle bag over MICHAEL's head, and then manhandles him over to the pouffe.)

RUAIRI: Now come on Frank –

FRANK: *(To RUAIRI.)* – if yer know what's good for yer!

(To MICHAEL.) I got some questions for yer. You're gonna answer those questions and if you don't answer them correctly, I'm gonna punch you like this.

(FRANK punches MICHAEL in the face. MICHAEL groans and collapses on the ground.)

Do you understand?

(Michael groans.)

Fucking say something!

RUAIRI: He's awful laconic, which often comes over as arrogance when in fact it's shyness.

(FRANK goes over to RUAIRI, close up.)

FRANK: I'm working. What am I fucking doing?

RUAIRI: Working.

(FRANK nuts RUAIRI bang on the nose. RUAIRI collapses on to the sofa holding his nose. RUAIRI starts wailing. FRANK hauls RUAIRI into the bathroom. And closes the door.)

RUAIRI: I'll stay in here Frank, I understand. Agh!

(FRANK goes back over to MICHAEL and manhandles him back on to the pouffe.)

FRANK: OK shy cunt. First question. What's the difference between a canal and a river?

MICHAEL: A canal is man made.

FRANK: Good. Yer see how easy these questions are? Next question. What was Popeye's favourite food.

MICHAEL: Tinned spinach.

FRANK: Tinned?

MICHAEL: I think it was always tinned.

FRANK: Aye. So. Did I punch yer that time shy cunt?

MICHAEL: No.

FRANK: Do you see how this works shy cunt?

MICHAEL: Yes.

FRANK: OK. Are you a tout for the Brits?

MICHAEL: If I answer truthfully, you're gonna punch me.

FRANK: If you tell the truth, I will not punch you.

MICHAEL: OK. I am not a tout for the Brits.

(FRANK punches him viciously. MICHAEL collapses forwards, groaning. FRANK hauls him up.)

RUAIRI: *(Off.)* None of us knew about the Eksund. Costello was the only one what knew!

(FRANK hauls the prostrate MICHAEL back into a kneeling position on the pouffe.)

FRANK: Doyle! Where was that ship loaded?

MICHAEL: Tripoli.

(FRANK punches him viciously and MICHAEL yells.)

RUAIRI: *(Off.)* What yer punch him for!? That's the right answer!

(FRANK takes a battery operated drill off the sofa. It had been wrapped in a towel in the duffle bag. It is fitted with a long drill bit. FRANK gives it a very short spin to check it's working. Then he goes over to the bathroom door.)

FRANK: *(Quietly.)* Ruairi? Can you hear me?

RUAIRI: *(Off.)* Yes, I'm sorry, I'll shut up.

FRANK: Can you hear me? I want to tell you something. But don't open the door.

RUAIRI: *(Off.)* OK, I can hear you.

(FRANK moves the drill bit to where he thinks RUAIRI's head might be, and drills through the thin quarter panel in one go. RUAIRI screams. During the next RUAIRI's screaming in the bathroom continues. FRANK goes over to MICHAEL and runs the drill near his ear, just so he can hear it. MICHAEL is now whimpering.)

FRANK: Is it the Brits you're talking with, or the FBI?

(FRANK runs the drill near MICHAEL's ear.)

MICHAEL: I'm not talking to anyone about anything.

(FRANK places the drill on MICHAEL's knee cap. COSTELLO opens the door with his own keys and enters. He closes the door behind him. COSTELLO slowly pulls out a small hand gun from his jacket pocket. He points it at FRANK.)

COSTELLO: Did you have a good flight?

FRANK: Cork to fucking Reykjavik. Fucking Reykjavik to fucking Toronto. Toronto to fucking JFK.

COSTELLO: That's the price of fame Frank McArdle. Get that drill outa the way.

(FRANK at first refuses to comply.)

How many men have you killed Frank?

FRANK: Seven.

COSTELLO: Fourteen.

(*FRANK complies, dropping the drill to one side.*)

Sit on the sofa.

(*FRANK complies. COSTELLO pulls the duffle bag off MICHAEL, revealing his beaten face.*)

This is no way to treat my people.

FRANK: One of you is a tout for the Brits.

(*COSTELLO goes over to the bathroom door. RUAIRI's moans can still be heard.*)

COSTELLO: You OK Ruairi?!

(*RUAIRI opens the door. He stands there not wanting to come out. The drill has grazed his shoulder and bloodied his shirt. It looks like he's been making a bit of a fuss. MICHAEL staggers to the bathroom to clean himself up as RUAIRI comes out.*)

RUAIRI: He tried to fucking kill me. The fucking psycho.

(*COSTELLO, with gun still out, sits in an armchair a safe distance from FRANK.*)

COSTELLO: What's the accusation?

FRANK: Someone betrayed that ship from Libya.

COSTELLO: I'm the only one in New York who knew about that shipment.

FRANK: You coulda told one of these two.

COSTELLO: So Security have sent you to insult and torture my people. Find out who it is, and kill them?

FRANK: Aye. How come you knew about the shipment when it was a secret?

COSTELLO: Secret? Bullshit. McGuiness briefed the executive. Has anyone in Ireland considered that it might be McGuinness himself who told the Brits? Or Gerry.

FRANK: The Big Lad? Hell would have to freeze over first.

COSTELLO: What would've happened if those hundred and fifty tons of arms had gotten through. Frank?

FRANK: We'da gone all out against the Brits.

COSTELLO: And every time we have intensified the war they stop voting for Sinn Fein. Am I right? It's not rocket science is it?

FRANK: How are yer gonna accuse them of that?

COSTELLO: I will fly to Dublin, and invite myself to be court martialed.

FRANK: That's a good idea, if you wanna die and be buried in Ireland.

COSTELLO: A court martial will give me a platform to say what needs to be said.

FRANK: I'll have to make a few phone calls.

COSTELLO: Michael! Did I not buy you an eighteen year old MacAllan single malt for Thanksgiving?

MICHAEL: You sure did.

COSTELLO: And you're saving it for the right girl?

RUAIRI: I know where he's fucking hiding it!

(RUAIRI goes into MICHAEL's bedroom.)

COSTELLO: I've heard you've been on the twelve step programme and gotten yourself clean of the drink.

FRANK: Aye.

COSTELLO: I tried that, yeah, I was a friend of Bill W once, but the drink won.

FRANK: "Keep coming back".

COSTELLO: Ha! Yeah, "keep coming back". Huh! And what the hell was that other one? "It's cunning"

FRANK: – It's "cunning, baffling and powerful."

COSTELLO: That's it. Your wife must be pleased?

FRANK: She said if I drink again, I'm out. And if I know one thing about meself it's that without her I'm lost.

COSTELLO: I forget her name

FRANK: Mary.

COSTELLO: And have you stopped beating her?

FRANK: Long time now. And how's your wife Mr. Costello?

(Beat.) And you got the one girl I think.

COSTELLO: We lost her.

FRANK: That's a bit fucking careless.

COSTELLO: She killed herself. Two months ago now.

FRANK: Slash her wrists? Hung herself? What?

COSTELLO: She'd been a heroin addict for years. Overdose.

FRANK: And she, your only one an'all.

(Enter MICHAEL from the bathroom cleaning himself up.)

MICHAEL: I would like you, sir, to shoot that fucking animal dead.

COSTELLO: Relax Michael. This is all part of the everyday push and pull of a people's volunteer army. Get some glasses. Four.

FRANK: I'll not be needing a glass.

COSTELLO: Four glasses please Michael.

(MICHAEL goes to get glasses. He comes back with four. RUAIRI comes in with the MACALLAN.)

RUAIRI: Ooh, I've been waiting for this day so!

COSTELLO: Do you know this malt Frank? Eighteen year old MacAllan, Scotch. My God man, this is, for me, the most beautiful single malt, and I'm gutted that it isn't Irish but hey…what do you do? A hundred and ten dollars a bottle. I bought it for Michael here, my friend and colleague, because I love him.

(COSTELLO opens the bottle. He sniffs the bottle. COSTELLO passes it under RUAIRI's nose.)

RUAIRI: Will yer give me a shot of that quick!

(COSTELLO gives the gun to MICHAEL. He then goes over to FRANK and passes the bottle under his nose. He lets it linger there. There is a hint of struggle.)

COSTELLO: Have you never had a slug of this label?

FRANK: No.

COSTELLO: Never had a shot of the best eh? You got well too soon buddy!

(They laugh.)

FRANK: I can see it's good, but I'm not drinking.

(COSTELLO pours a good measure in front of him into what is ostensibly FRANK's glass.)

COSTELLO: I bet you gave your life away to two cent brands, grain whiskies, blends. Shit! And now, even though you can see it before you, you can't taste it.

(COSTELLO pours for MICHAEL. He drinks.)

MICHAEL: Hell!

COSTELLO: Can you taste the money?

(MICHAEL stands.)

MICHAEL: Ladies and Gentlemen! We've just crossed the border!

(They laugh.)

COSTELLO: Michael's usually a quiet guy. In ten minutes I'll have his personality on the stage and I'll be selling fucking tickets.

RUAIRI: Me! Me! Me!

(COSTELLO serves a drink to RUAIRI. RUAIRI drinks, and slowly savours.)

RUAIRI: Christ! That could give a dead man the horn.

(COSTELLO pours for himself. And drinks. He says nothing.)

COSTELLO: You don't mind us drinking in front of you?

FRANK: Do what the fuck yer like.

COSTELLO: Do you want a soda?

FRANK: Glass of water.

COSTELLO: Ruairi! A glass of water for this family man farmer.

RUAIRI: Aye, aye.

(RUAIRI complies.)

COSTELLO: How did you used to drink your whisky Frank?

FRANK: Bit of ice.

COSTELLO: I like a bit of rattle in the glass that's true. Ice for Frank's whiskey.

(RUAIRI complies. Silence. FRANK stares at the glass. It looks like he might drink but he doesn't. RUAIRI delivers a glass of water to FRANK and puts ice in.)

FRANK: I don't want ice in my water.

COSTELLO: I thought maybe you can drink water with ice and maybe you can imagine you're drinking a double on the rocks.

RUAIRI: *(Drinking.)* Beautiful.

COSTELLO: How's the war going Frank?

FRANK: We need Stinger missiles. Can you get us a Stinger? Qaddafi's outa the picture now.

COSTELLO: And your way of persuading me to bust my balls to get you a Stinger is to come over here and humiliate my people?

FRANK: It's not my job to ask for Stingers.

Costello: I guess for that they'll send someone more respectful. I can get you a Stinger. You know, I used to read Grainne, off to sleep, kiss her goodnight, when she was a kid, back in the seventies, back when we were busy

MICHAEL: – Packing them Armalites through the night.

COSTELLO: I don't know if you read your children off to sleep Frank?

FRANK: Aye, I do. I did.

COSTELLO: But there's always that moment when you're still reading and they're already asleep, and yer look at them and wonder at their beauty, and their innocence.

FRANK: Aye.

COSTELLO: And I guess before you leave them to the dark, you check they're still breathing. Do you do that Frank?

FRANK: Aye. I did. Aye.

COSTELLO: I imagine that that is what every father has always done. Leaving Grainne's room I had to pass a mirror and look at myself, and for me, that was a difficult moment, because that year, after Bloody Sunday, there were five hundred killed in my war, dead by my rifles. And I had to be strong in that moment, like you are now with the drink, so that I didn't slip down into doubt. What has kept me going all these years is a bright, clear, unequivocal shaft of light – a sure knowledge that our war is a just war.

(COSTELLO walks behind FRANK. He is holding the whisky bottle.)

You see, Frank, unlike you, I'm not mentally ill. I don't do this shit for fun. You've got a fucking nerve coming to my country to abuse and physically assault my people. You're not a soldier. You think soldiering is about violence, don't you? War requires, the first thing it fucking requires, is a clear moral purpose!

FRANK: I don't know what the fuck you're on about.

COSTELLO: They call me the Big Fellah, over here. I like it. I godda weakness for that kind of shit. But do you know who the real Big Fellah is?

FRANK: No. I don't.

COSTELLO: Gordon Wilson, … I mean can you think of a more British name.

FRANK: *(Weak.)* And who the fuck is Gordon Wilson?

COSTELLO: We killed his daughter at Enniskillen…and he is big, and gracious enough not to hate us for it, and said as much on TV. And if he were here now I would hold him in my arms, and I would tell him that I too have lost a daughter, and that I am praying for his girl, the girl my army killed, and I would tell him that he is as good and true an Irishman as any that ever pulled on boots. *(Beat.)* So Frank, tell me, as a member of the IRA council of war, you fucking tell me right now what moral purpose there is in the cold blooded murder of six women on Remembrance Sunday as they stand by the graves of their sons and husbands long dead!?

(COSTELLO pours whisky into his hand and rubs it into FRANK's face and hair.)

Speak or drink.

(FRANK grabs his arm.)

Let go my arm. Shoot him dead Michael.

(FRANK lets the arm go.)

OK. Hold it.

(COSTELLO tilts FRANK's head back and opens his mouth. He then pours the whisky into his open mouth. During the next, FRANK drinks in this way. Then COSTELLO comes round the sofa and sits. FRANK leans forward and drinks from his glass. COSTELLO tops FRANK's glass up. COSTELLO fills up everyone's drinks. They drink. FRANK drinks, is topped up, drinks again, then sobs. The others drink.)

Keep coming back Frank. Keep coming back.

FADE TO BLACK

SCENE 2

(A different art gallery.)

KARELMA: Frank McArdle's been over.

RUAIRI: You know?

KARELMA: Sure.

RUAIRI: He's talking to the Big Fellah about gear and that.

KARELMA: OK.

RUAIRI: Stingers.

KARELMA: It's what you need.

RUAIRI: Aye, imagine one Stinger in South Armagh. The Brits'd couldn't move the grunts around so the county would be ours.

KARELMA: Can Costello get Stingers?

RUAIRI: Oh aye. And there's a move to divorce Sinn Fein and start a new army, and Costello's all for that. Which is a shock to me cos I thought he was sick of the whole business with his daughter, and now his wife's walked out on him.

KARELMA: We know.

RUAIRI: Course yer do. His house'll be broadcasting twenty four hours a day, eh? Do yer listen to us at Michael's?

KARELMA: What do you think?

RUAIRI: I don't care. I wouldn't take a woman back there. I've never been able to give you very much have I, they know I can't keep my mouth shut so they don't tell me nothing. Costello's very low. Never seen him this bad. Except for being very keen to get the Stingers, which is strange.

KARELMA: With Qaddafi out the picture it's a chance to get his war back. Do you know where he would go for his Stingers?

RUAIRI: I do not.

KARELMA: Ruairi, you're being a bit, I dunno, cool with me.

RUAIRI: I don't want paying no more. I got me qualifications, and this new job is a whole lot of money, and I'm moving outa Woodlawn, gonna get me own place downtown.

KARELMA: Are you still gonna talk to me?

RUAIRI: Aye, but I don't want yer owning me no more. I sold yer me soul, and done alright by it, with the visa and the money and that, but I have to work out if I can enjoy the rest of me life, knowing what I done. You *not paying me*, will help with that.

KARELMA: That's an unusual arrangement.

RUAIRI: I still want a free state, and the Brits out, and all the rest of the stuff I've always wanted. I just wished we could do it without anyone ever getting a nosebleed. I'm trapped on the inside with them cos no-one leaves the IRA, and I'm tied to you cos I need your protection. One of these nights yer gonna get a desperate phone call from yer old friend Ruairi O'Drisceoil, yer know that don't yer? Yer gonna have to get me out. And to do that yer gonna have to act pretty fucking quick.

KARELMA: Sure.

RUAIRI: A new name?

KARELMA: Yeah.

RUAIRI: Do I get to choose?

KARELMA: No.

RUAIRI: OK. Can you do what you can to avoid "Humphrey"?

KARELMA: It ain't me that does the choosing.

RUAIRI: And if I got a woman with me?

KARELMA: Congratulations.

RUAIRI: I haven't done the decent thing yet mind. Do you need to know her name?

KARELMA: Sure do.

RUAIRI: Stella Tomaszewski. She's not Irish.

KARELMA: OK. It would help if you're married.

RUAIRI: Understand. Fucking hell don't rush me into stuff.

KARELMA: Sure.

RUAIRI: You know way back, that first St. Patrick's Day, when I kissed you in the pub, and took you home to mine, was you FBI back then?

KARELMA: Sorry, yeah, I was getting paid.

RUAIRI: Not enough obviously, or I woulda got me leg over. OK. Another one. I've been giving you information for six years now, and Tom Billy hasn't even had a knock on the door. Michael. Costello. The bombs keep going off, like I tell yer they will, and it's all as if I'm blabbing away to me barber, and not the FBI.

KARELMA: I've passed on everything you've ever told me. But ya godda understand the Irish got a lot of clout. If it's a firehouse or the Whitehouse – it helps if you're Irish.

(Beat.) If you make that phone call, where would you wanna go?

RUAIRI: Ireland.

KARELMA: (Laughs)

RUAIRI: Aye, it's fucking hilarious isn't it.

KARELMA: You gonna run an Irish music festival?

RUAIRI: Take the piss, go on. I've got an ache inside for the auld bog, and it's the only place in the world where I don't stick out like a sore thumb.

KARELMA: *(Still amused.)* OK.

RUAIRI: And I might come to terms with what I done. And I don't mean talking to you. When I shot that young lad, the British soldier –

KARELMA: – you shot him? We thought you were the driver.

RUAIRI: I shot him. Me.

(RUAIRI is cracking up.)

Get me back to Ireland. If I can build a grand, proud, useful building, and cast some new fucking shadow on this earth at least I've done something.

End of scene.

Act 4

(1998.)

SCENE 1

(The Woodlawn apartment. May 1998. TOM BILLY COYLE, RUAIRI, and MICHAEL. TOM BILLY COYLE is out of uniform, in casuals. He's put on weight. They're drinking. It's evening. They're waiting for COSTELLO. RUAIRI's accent is more and more New York.)

RUAIRI: Ah, you're full of shit, Tom Billy! Those pull boxes are beautiful, iconic, and functional, and a part of New York. If you don't have a telephone and you're on fire, you just go out on to the street and tug the handle of a pull box and you can talk to the emergency services. Brilliant. Someone who might not have a phone, an example might be if yer deaf.

TOM BILLY: Fuck the deaf! Fuck 'em! Who gives a fuck! Why should I bust my ass on these streets, risking my fucking life for a few deaf assholes!

RUAIRI: I see that tolerance training programme you went on has finally kicked in.

TOM BILLY: Fuck 'em!

MICHAEL: Ninety percent of those 10 – 75s are bullshit.

TOM BILLY: Bullshit!

MICHAEL: They are.

TOM BILLY: I'm agreeing with you lieutenant! They're all bullshit! What makes me puke is that we make it easy for them! We put a fucking pull box on the corner of every block in – (every fucking project.)

MICHAEL: – every two blocks.

TOM BILLY: – paint the motherfucker red, stick an ice cream on the top

MICHAEL: – that's not an icecream Tom Billy, that's meant to be a torch, a flame.

TOM BILLY: Fuck you lieutenant! Do you think I do not know that?

MICHAEL: Quit the lieutenant will ya.

TOM BILLY: There it is punk! Lit up in lights, pull the handle and in ten minutes you'll have your own private NYPD, FDNY Barnum and Bailey fucking street circus!

RUAIRI: I sympathise with the deaf. I might be deaf myself one day! Listening to you Tom Billy!

TOM BILLY: Funny guy!

MICHAEL: Get a cell phone.

TOM BILLY: It's nineteen ninety eight LOSER! If your deaf ass is on fire ring nine one one!

RUAIRI: I know it's difficult for you Tom Billy but if you empathise a little

TOM BILLY: – "empathise". Are you gay?

RUAIRI: *(Shouting.)* IF YER DEAF! – it's not so easy to use a telephone, on account of your inability to hear what the other party is saying.

TOM BILLY: Bullshit!

RUAIRI: That's not bullshit! That's the very definition of deafness, you big lump of fucking muscle!

TOM BILLY: What are you Ruairi? A fucking dumbass architect, a paper chaser –

RUAIRI: – Now you're going to tell me I know nothing about life!

TOM BILLY: Jack shit! Watch out for the paper cuts man!

RUAIRI: I only design buildings, ipso facto – I don't see life in the raw, and consequently end up a fucking LIBERAL! If I were a cop, of course, I would spend all day on the streets flicking bits of dead mugger's brains off of me sandwiches and would, over time, accumulate an intelligence born of experience resulting in wise observations like FUCK THE DEAF!

TOM BILLY: *(Stands.)* Fuck you citizen! You fucking wannabe artist!

RUAIRI: Did I abuse you when you were a wannabe comedian?

TOM BILLY: You sure did asshole!

RUAIRI: *(To MICHAEL.)* Do you know what he wants to do with the homeless?

TOM BILLY: Target practice.

RUAIRI: You're sick in the head!

(MICHAEL laughs. TOM BILLY mimes a few pistol shots.)

TOM BILLY: Where does it say in the constitution of America that it's OK to spend your life sitting on the fucking sidewalk outside Pizza Hut on your fat lazy ass tied to a cross bred mongrel?!

RUAIRI: I'd like you now to slag off the Muslim terrorists. To be here now, awaiting orders for our own little war in the North, and to listen to you riffing on about the barbarism of the towel heads could be wonderfully ironic.

TOM BILLY: Muslims?

RUAIRI: Yes, Muslims, and Tom Billy…don't hold yourself back!

TOM BILLY: Are you serious?! You fucking what? You mental defective. You can't compare what we're doing with what those fucking cavemen want?!

RUAIRI: More, more!

MICHAEL: What do they want?

TOM BILLY: The fucking guy who tried to blow up the World Trade Centre?!

RUAIRI: This is better than television!

MICHAEL: What do they want? I don't get it.

TOM BILLY: Those guys are all fucked in the head man!

RUAIRI: Are they evil!?

TOM BILLY: Fuck you citizen! He said he wanted to kill two hundred and fifty thousand people!

MICHAEL: Innocent people.

RUAIRI: And we only murder the guilty!

TOM BILLY: He blew that truck up in the basement. He was tryna bring the fucking towers down. Can you imagine that? Can you imagine if he'd brought the towers down!? The fucking world trade centre! Man! Imagine that!

RUAIRI: *(Laughing.)* You can't see it can yer!

MICHAEL: What is it they want? That's what I don't get.

TOM BILLY: They want the whole fucking world to eat humus!

(Beat.)

(Serious.) They nearly killed me that day.

RUAIRI: Of course it's all about you isn't it Tom Billy?!

TOM BILLY: February 26th nineteen ninety – what was it?

RUAIRI: – ninety three

MICHAEL: – how many times have you told us this story!?

TOM BILLY: – that day, I was working that precinct.

RUAIRI: You were the main target Tom Billy!

TOM BILLY: Fuck you!

MICHAEL: The bomb was lunchtime. You were on nights!

TOM BILLY: Yeah, sure, I was on nights.

RUAIRI: But they weren't to know that! How could they know that he was tucked up in bed in Queens with his hand on his cock?! You out fooled them there Tom Billy!

TOM BILLY: Eat shit asshole!

MICHAEL: They gave no warnings man. That's immoral!

TOM BILLY: We give warnings.

RUAIRI: Ah yes! The "exemplar" terrorist bombing is the way we do it, like Enniskillen!

MICHAEL: Enniskillen was a fuck up.

TOM BILLY: And... we apologised.

MICHAEL: You can't draw anything from Enniskillen.

TOM BILLY: We should nuke the whole fucking Middle East. Look at the way they treat their women!

MICHAEL: I don't understand what they want.

TOM BILLY: They want the dark ages man. They wanna turn all the fucking lights off.

RUAIRI: But I would guess Tom Billy that you would sympathise with their approach to the thorny issue of the gay community.

(MICHAEL laughs.)

TOM BILLY: What are you laughing at?

MICHAEL: He's got you there.

RUAIRI: They wanna chuck all the gays off the mountain, and lordy lordy so do you Tom Billy!

TOM BILLY: Some of my best friends are members of the gay community!

(TOM BILLY does a Pinnochio nose. MICHAEL laughs.)

Gay community. What the fuck is that? A "community" is where you can knock on the door and say "excuse me, can you lend me a bowl of sugar please?". In a faggot community you get a knock on the door and the guy says "can you lend me a bowl of sugar please? and if you've got a minute spare do you mind nailing my dick to the wardrobe!"

MICHAEL: He's doing old material.

RUAIRI: It wasn't funny then and it isn't funny now…

TOM BILLY: All that federal money to "AIDS VICTIMS". Victims? Fuck you! If your idea of a good weekend is fucking fifteen strangers up the ass then sooner or later buddy you're gonna catch a cold!

RUAIRI: Have you ever slept with a man Tom Billy?

(MICHAEL laughs.)

TOM BILLY: Fuck you!

RUAIRI: I blew a guy once.

(Silence.)

A telephone engineer from Boulder, Colorado.

MICHAEL: You gave a telephone engineer from Boulder Colorado a blow job?

RUAIRI: Yeah.

TOM BILLY: Why did you do that?

RUAIRI: It felt like the decent thing to do.

MICHAEL: Why?

RUAIRI: Cos he'd just given me one.

TOM BILLY: Wow! I always sympathised with you Ruairi, ya
know the way your street started getting a name as the
place to go in Midtown East where you could pick up
some junky piece of shit faggot, well, I declined to call it
what it was and I always referred to it as 53rd and 3rd but
now I know you're gay too, I'm gonna go back to calling it
O'Drisceoil corner. Faggot!

*(TOM BILLY and RUAIRI stand aggressively. TOM BILLY throws an
empty can at RUAIRI. RUAIRI picks up a can and throws it at TOM
BILLY. MICHAEL stands between them.)*

MICHAEL: Hey guys! Cool it.

TOM BILLY: I'm NYPD ya know. I can have you thrown outa
my country. Are you legal yet? Is he legal?

MICHAEL: He's been legal fifteen years Tom Billy. You don't
listen.

RUAIRI: Cos you're DEAF!

(TOM BILLY sits.)

TOM BILLY: Where the fuck is Costello?! Huh? Is he coming?
He wants us to do some packing, yeah?

MICHAEL: I do not know.

TOM BILLY: Packing. We're gonna be packing all night.

MICHAEL: He's late, that's all I know.

TOM BILLY: Is it packing? Maybe it's an operation.

RUAIRI: Yeah, big guy, you godda kill another woman.

TOM BILLY: Fuck you man!

RUAIRI: Agh!

(TOM BILLY flies across the room and pins RUAIRI to the floor. MICHAEL dives in and separates them. They're all on the floor. TOM BILLY gets one punch in on RUAIRI.)

MICHAEL: Guys! Quit! Hell!

TOM BILLY: D'ya hear him. D'ya hear what he said?!

MICHAEL: I heard him. Now cool it guys. Ruairi, cool it.

RUAIRI: You punched me. In the mouth.

TOM BILLY: I had orders. Jerk.

MICHAEL: He had orders. You know he had orders.

RUAIRI: What? To punch me?

MICHAEL: To kill the girl.

RUAIRI: To kill your girl.

(MICHAEL punches RUAIRI.)

RUAIRI: Agh! You punched me now!

(RUAIRI stands and goes to the bathroom, and goes in, closing the door behind him.)

TOM BILLY: This might be Aids blood. Ah, Jesus.

MICHAEL: Hell, did I punch Ruairi?

TOM BILLY: Yeah.

MICHAEL: Shit.

TOM BILLY: We got a tout ya know. Godda be. One of us. Look at the Stinger operation. Chuck and Francis got four years for that. That whole thing was an FBI set up.

MICHAEL: Costello?

TOM BILLY: It ain't me. That ship an'all. Way back. It ain't me man.

MICHAEL: Ruairi?

TOM BILLY: When did he get his Green Card?

MICHAEL: He's been legal years.

TOM BILLY: I looked on the computer man. He's godda criminal record in Ireland. No way you're gonna get legal with a record like that. Unless you get help.

MICHAEL: What are you saying?

TOM BILLY: It ain't me. That's all I'm saying.

(RUAIRI comes out of the bathroom, nursing his mouth.)

RUAIRI: *(To TOM BILLY.)* Yer fucking punched me. Yer a violent man.

(To MICHAEL.) And you punched me an'all. And you're not a violent man.

He's the nutter.

(Enter COSTELLO. He has his own keys. He is carrying two or three big laundry bags packed with folded down cardboard boxes, Teddy Bears in boxes, and boxed up FX401 detonators.)

TOM BILLY: *(Looking at the bags.)* Packing. Didn't I tell ya?

COSTELLO: How's it going?

TOM BILLY: Ruairi's telling us about his faggot weekends.

RUAIRI: I blew a guy once Mr. Costello.

COSTELLO: You blew a guy?

RUAIRI: Yeah.

COSTELLO: Why d'yer do that?

RUAIRI: I was having no success with the ladies.

COSTELLO: Did you kiss him on the lips?

RUAIRI: I did not, no.

COSTELLO: That's alright then.

RUAIRI: Thank you.

COSTELLO: Was this before you met your wife?

RUAIRI: Stella.

COSTELLO: Of course, Stella.

RUAIRI: Yeah and she knows about it.

TOM BILLY: Shit man! He's told his wife. Fucking liberals!

(*RUAIRI hands over a flyer to COSTELLO.*)

RUAIRI: This is an invitation for my private view –

TOM BILLY: *(Gay stereotype.)* – "my private view". Cocksucker!

COSTELLO: You know I wanna buy that one that's a bit like a Mondrian.

RUAIRI: They're all a bit like Mondrian.

TOM BILLY: Fuck, will you cut me some slack here guys!? I'm blue collar, I can't listen to shit like this, I'm gonna chuck.

MICHAEL: Let me get you a drink Mr. Costello.

TOM BILLY: We're celebrating.

RUAIRI: Michael's made lieutenant at last.

TOM BILLY: *(With a giggle.)* Sixth attempt.

COSTELLO: A quitter never wins, and a winner never quits! Lieutenant, wow.

MICHAEL: Ladder 15. Water Street.

COSTELLO: Near the river, near South Street?

MICHAEL: Yeah.

COSTELLO: OK. We must lunch, I'm often in Lower Manhattan.

MICHAEL: I don't get a lunch like that.

COSTELLO: Well done Michael. Good for the pension, huh?

MICHAEL: Hey, don't talk like that.

TOM BILLY: What are we packing?

COSTELLO: FX 401s.

TOM BILLY: Detonators.

RUAIRI: We're gonna blow something?

TOM BILLY: Not you. You've blown enough!

COSTELLO: One big something yeah.

(MICHAEL has taken a Teddy out the box.)

MICHAEL: Teddy Bears! Cute!

COSTELLO: We got to get these FX 401s through customs. We stuff each detonator in a Teddy, and let the post man do the rest.

RUAIRI: "Neither rain, nor snow, nor sleet, nor hail, shall keep the postmen from their appointed rounds".

MICHAEL: Air mail.

RUAIRI: These addresses can't be Real IRA.

COSTELLO: Sympathisers. They're expecting the Teddy's. We only need one to get through. Take out the voice box.

(TOM BILLY presses the voice box. The Teddy says "I love you Mummy!" Or similar.)

MICHAEL: Cute.

(TOM BILLY takes out the voice box by opening the velcro/zip back on the Teddy.)

Replace with an FX 401.

(TOM BILLY complies.)

Pack it.

MICHAEL: If customs scan the box they'll think the electrical kit is the Teddy's voice box.

RUAIRI: OK lieutenant, we worked that out.

TOM BILLY: OK, let's go.

(TOM BILLY drags the bags on to the coffee table and takes out a pile of Teddy Bears in boxes, and various boxes of switches – branded FX401. The production line is as follows – TOM BILLY pulls out from the back of a Teddy Bear the electronic voice box. He then passes the gutted Teddy Bear along to MICHAEL who sticks one of the FX401 switches in its place. This then goes down the line to be packed and addressed.)

MICHAEL: Sit there Mr. Costello.

COSTELLO: *(With a piece of paper in his hand.)* Who wants the addresses?

TOM BILLY/MICHAEL: Ruairi.

TOM BILLY: Women's work. Ha, ha!

RUAIRI: Cos it's real man's work, ripping the guts out of a big hairy arsed Teddy Bear and way beyond the likes of a nine stone weakling with artistic inclinations.

(MICHAEL places in front of RUAIRI the first Teddy Bear which needs packing. RUAIRI just stares at it.)

RUAIRI: What's the target?

TOM BILLY: Pack the fucking Teddy Bear cock sucker!

COSTELLO: Pack the Teddy Bear Ruairi.

RUAIRI: No. I wanna know. What's the target?

TOM BILLY: Pack the Teddy punk!

RUAIRI: Is it a military target?

COSTELLO: It's not military.

RUAIRI: I'm not packing.

TOM BILLY: Pack the fucking Teddy Bear soldier!

RUAIRI: It's not military!

TOM BILLY: Who – (gives a fuck.)

COSTELLO: – Tom Billy! Shutup.

(TOM BILLY shuts up and sits down.)

Michael: (Laughs.)

TOM BILLY: What are you laughing at?

COSTELLO: It's an operation against those who support the Good Friday Peace Agreement.

TOM BILLY: We're gonna blow up the Pope?

COSTELLO: It's not the Pope.

TOM BILLY: Me and the Pope got a lot in common. He don't like wearing a rubber and neither do I.

RUAIRI: Are we gonna hit Adams?

COSTELLO: It's not Adams.

TOM BILLY: We should be hitting Adams. Shit! I bust my ass for twenty years for Gerry Adams, a fucking lifetime, and when he finally gets a visa, when he finally comes to my town –

RUAIRI: – this ain't your town.

TOM BILLY: – this town fucking is my town!

(To COSTELLO.) When he finally comes to my town how come you don't get invited to lunch at the Sheraton huh? How come Adams ain't saying "thank you" to our Mister Costello, publicly, knowhatimean?

COSTELLO: There was only one seat at the table. It was either me or Clinton.

MICHAEL: I heard they shook hands.

RUAIRI: Of course they shook hands.

TOM BILLY: Shake hands? Fuck you. Gerry Adams got his dick out, and Clinton blew him. Forget Monica whatshername –

(Some of them laugh.)

MICHAEL: – Lewinsky.

TOM BILLY: Forget Monica Lewinsky, the real scandal is that the President of America flew into my town on Airforce One and blew Gerry Adams at the Sheraton in front of Kissinger.

(MICHAEL is laughing now. RUAIRI giggling.)

TOM BILLY: And the scandal is that we, our organisation, him, we were not represented at the function, the blowing event, when it was us that made that event possible.

COSTELLO: So what do you want to do about it Tom Billy?

TOM BILLY: Stormont. The castle. Boof! *(He mimes an explosion.)*

COSTELLO: It's not Stormont.

RUAIRI: If it's not Adams, not military or political, what is it?

COSTELLO: I can't tell you.

RUAIRI: OK. I understand but I'm not touching anything.

(RUAIRI stands, and raises his hands away from the Teddys.)

(To COSTELLO.) After Enniskillen, you told me, you promised me we would only go for the Brits. Military. You, yourself, I heard you say that!

COSTELLO: I have orders from the new people – (I)

RUAIRI: No! I never believed that about you. That you take orders. You're your own man Mr. Costello. What's the target?

TOM BILLY: He can't fucking tell you, dumbass.

COSTELLO: It's an attack on the peace process. It's a commercial target.

RUAIRI: Commercial?

MICHAEL: What's commercial?

TOM BILLY: A shop. A protestant shop. Marks and Spencers. No, they're Jewish. We don't want to do that I'm one eighth Jewish.

MICHAEL: You're an eighth Jewish?

TOM BILLY: I'm Brooklyn ain't I. Everyone in Brooklyn's at least one eighth Jewish.

COSTELLO: What do people do when there's peace? They go shopping.

RUAIRI: So we're gonna blow up some women and kids when they're out shopping? I got family all over Ireland. Which town?

TOM BILLY: He can't tell you. Don't tell him sir.

MICHAEL: It ain't gonna be County Cork.

RUAIRI: I got family in the north.

COSTELLO: Omagh.

TOM BILLY: You told him.

RUAIRI: You told me this Real IRA we joined was gonna be an army. I'm out.

TOM BILLY: You're fucking in man.

RUAIRI: I'm out. I said. I'm out.

TOM BILLY: There's in and there's Mexico. OK?

RUAIRI: Yeah, yeah – you threaten me. Go ahead. I'm out.

(RUAIRI stands and makes his way to the door. TOM BILLY follows him. And puts himself between RUAIRI and the door.)

COSTELLO: Tom Billy's right Ruairi. There is no out I'm afraid.

RUAIRI: I'm out.

TOM BILLY: Can he go?

MICHAEL: Let him go.

TOM BILLY: Can we let him go? Sir?!

COSTELLO: Let him go.

(RUAIRI leaves.)

TOM BILLY: We'll get orders. Yeah? On Ruairi.

COSTELLO: Yeah.

MICHAEL: You think?

COSTELLO: Yeah.

MICHAEL: Do they have to know? We don't have to say. Sir?

COSTELLO: We do have to say.

MICHAEL: Shit.

TOM BILLY: Of course we'll get fucking orders.

COSTELLO: We'll wait.

(COSTELLO takes over RUAIRI's job, packing, wrapping, addressing etc.)

TOM BILLY: We think Ruairi's been informing.

COSTELLO: Yeah?

MICHAEL: The Stingers operation was a set up.

COSTELLO: And what information did he have about that? None.

TOM BILLY: He got a criminal record in Ireland so how's he get a green card? Huh?

COSTELLO: If Ruairi was a tout we'd all be in the Lincoln Correctional.

TOM BILLY: That ain't how it works Mr. Costello. The FBI, and the Brits, they get someone on the inside, they keep them there. They get the info, they don't bust the unit.

MICHAEL: Why don't they bust the unit?

TOM BILLY: If they bust the unit, then we'd start a new unit, which they wouldn't know anything about.

COSTELLO: Leave it to me, Tom Billy, and pass me that knife will you?

(They work.)

MICHAEL: We were talking earlier sir. What do these Muslims want? Ya know, if we give in and say "OK, OK ya got it! You can have what you want.

TOM BILLY: What the fuck do we give them?

MICHAEL: What do they want?

COSTELLO: Are you religious?

TOM BILLY: Catholic. No. Ya know. I like Christmas.

COSTELLO: They want what all religions want. They wanna punish us all for being human.

(Beat.) Gimme some packing tape.

Fade

SCENE 2

(The art gallery. RUAIRI sits and makes a phone call.)

RUAIRI: *(On the phone.)* Karelma? …it's me, …yeah… there's gonna be an operation… we've been shipping detonators…civilian target…Omagh, County Tyrone …I don't know….I don't know! Fuck!…and you gotta get me

out now. Now! Like right now, now… Anywhere you say.
But fucking now!

SCENE 3

*(Costello isolated in a spot, as in Act One Scene One. It is the 1999 St.
Patrick's Day Parade dinner. Buzz of laughter, talk, cutlery. COSTELLO
in a suit, not Brian Boru, now aged 64, stands, with a smile, gestures
with his hand, a blast of the pipes follows, silence.)*

COSTELLO: Thank you Jerry. Jerry has got a new book out "Learn
to play the pipes in one hour". Yeah, after just one hour you can
be as good Jerry.

(Laughter.)

Can you hear me at the back? One year I said that,
someone shouted out "I can hear, but I'm happy to swap
with someone who can't".

(Laughter.)

St. Patrick's day is a great day for the Irish.

(Cheers.)

It's even better if you're not Irish.

(Laughter.)

If you've spent the day pretending to be Irish you just get
up the next morning, say your apologies, forget the tears
and the pain, and go back to being Korean.

(Laughter.)

I would like you to put your hands together for our chef,
Wei Chang Lao, for a terrific meal!

(Applause.)

One of the benefits of peace in the north is that a plate of
food at this dinner now costs a helluva lot less.

(Laughter.)

My forefathers left Ireland in 1872. Some of the younger contenders for Parade Grand Marshal have started a rumour that I was with them.

(Laughter.)

This year, 1999, I will step aside and give them what they want – I'm resigning after twenty nine years.

(Applause. Everyone stands.)

I have, in the past, been keen to take your money.

(Laughter.)

Put your cheques away… I have no use for them. Thank God. I know most of you… I've held your babies, I've been there when you buried your dead…hell! how many times have I walked through Queens behind black horses?! We're family, yeah? I'm an intelligent man, though flawed obviously, and I know what you're thinking, sitting there, looking at me, wondering if there'll be any new jokes this year.

(Some laughter.)

– two snails on the freeway, tearing along, about eighty five miles an hour, they overtake this speedcop, one snail on the outside, one on the inside, …

(He stops. They wait for the punch line but he doesn't give it. Something weird going on…)

…the Irish built the prisons in this country, and then proceeded to fill them!

(Several laughs.)

That's an old one, one of Ronald Reagan's.

(One laugh.)

I've given you twenty years of jokes, you've had jokes enough.

I got a shock for you tonight. I'm not Irish, you're not Irish. I'm an American. Why is it not enough to be merely human? Why was it not enough for me to be born in Burlington New Jersey within a spit of the Tucker's Island light. Get over it. I am a man that's all. If that's not enough, to be an American, before you've even started you got a problem. I am sixteen, I come to New York, I meet a girl, the Grand Colleen of the 1952 parade. She is extraordinary. She falls in love with me!? Most men coulda filled a life loving her.

(Angry with himself now.)

I have a business, I have a wife, who loves me, we have a daughter, I'm a father. And that is not enough for me?! The axis of the earth, you know, that it's slightly out of whack, tilt yeah, that annoys me. Understand what I'm saying?

(Silence.)

What I did, and you all know what I did, at one time, was selfish. I so wanted to be The Big Fellah.

(Getting increasingly difficult for him.)

I was in the K Mart in Astor Place, ya know Lafayette and Broadway, I was buying insoles, yeah, for my shoes, and this woman, Puerto Rican… we went for a coffee at the Starbucks there…and I was at a low point in my life after Enniskillen, and Theresa and you know Graunia…they're clever like that, they knew that money wouldna tempted me, so they waited until I was weak, very clever. We, as Americans, should be proud of their professionalism of the FBI. Huh!? So many mistakes as a boy, and I thought at some point the mistake making would end…so…yes…I have been working for the FBI for the past twelve years.

(He takes a drink. There is nothing, no murmurs, just silence.)

The worst is to have lived a lie to you guys, my friends who have traveled with me. I thought you would have left by now. I rehearsed this speech, I always do. The stuff that looks off the cuff – yeah, well it's written down, mostly, rehearsed, the trick is to make it look not rehearsed.

(Increasingly difficult for him.)

Theresa would listen to me rehearsing. Laugh. Get me to change something. Thank you, thank you all, for being quiet, respectful. Maybe you acknowledge that, to admit publicly to the betrayal of friends is one man taking the hard road and facing up to what he has become. But this is another flaw, they call it "vanity". I want you to say – "he coulda just gone into hiding"; "No! the Big Fellah doesn't do things that way".

TOM BILLY: *(Off.)* You're a dead guy!

(Silence.)

COSTELLO: There was a time when I was confident and could deal with a little heckle.

TOM BILLY: *(Off.)* I said…you're a dead guy!

COSTELLO: *(Taking out a piece of paper.)* I would like to read a verse of a poem. Yeats.

(COSTELLO reads. He needs to read, he doesn't know it by heart.)

COSTELLO: I will arise and go now, and go to Innisfree –

TOM BILLY: *(Off.)* You're a dead guy.

COSTELLO: And a small cabin build there, of clay and wattles made –

TOM BILLY: *(Off.)* You're a dead guy.

COSTELLO: Nine bean rows will I have there, a hive for the honey bee –

TOM BILLY: *(Off.)* You're a dead guy.

COSTELLO: And live alone in the bee-loud glade –

(Beat.)

And I shall have some peace there, for peace comes dropping slow.

(Silence.)

IRISH VOICE: *(Off.)* We're gonna fucking burn you down!

Snap to Black

SCENE 4

(The Woodlawn flat. TOM BILLY and MICHAEL just home from the dinner, still dressed in kilts and ceremonials.)

MICHAEL: I think we should wait.

TOM BILLY: We don't need no orders. I'm gonna go up Oceanside now. Ya coming with me!

MICHAEL: He won'ta gone back to Long Beach. Not after that.

TOM BILLY: Jesus! I can't believe we let him outa the hall! Someone held me back. Big old guy, face like a fucking map, d'yer see him –

MICHAEL: – I saw him.

TOM BILLY: D'yer know him? I'll fucking waste him too.

MICHAEL: I been introduced to all those old timers, I don't remember their names.

TOM BILLY: Give me a clean gun. I ain't gonna use my Glock. What you got? Come on! Fuck!

MICHAEL: What do you want?

TOM BILLY: You got a Smith snub nose?

MICHAEL: Yeah.

TOM BILLY: That'll do nicely! Dig it up then Michael! Come on man! I got a licence! For fuck's sake, what's the matter wid you boy!?

(MICHAEL goes to the door, takes out his keys and locks the door, taking the keys out of the lock. He then finds an electric screwdriver, rolls back a bit of carpet and starts taking up a floorboard.)

It was the Big Fellah all along. Christ! And we were gonna Mexico Ruairi!

MICHAEL: We're still waiting on orders for Ruairi.

TOM BILLY: Fuck it man, he's gone. I coulda sworn it was Ruairi. I miss him. He was funny. Funny bones. You know if Ruairi had been doing my material, you know my material and his funny bones, I coulda made it, you know, as a comedy writer.

MICHAEL: It might have been Ruairi, as well.

TOM BILLY: Two touts in one team?! No way. You gotta come with me, you know the house. I don't want to make a mistake. It wouldn't be right to shoot the neighbours.

MICHAEL: I've only been to the house once, a barbecue.

TOM BILLY: Me, never. He never gave me nothing. Not even a dangerously undercooked piece of chicken. You go down Rockaway Boulevard and do a left towards Woodmere. Yeah?

MICHAEL: Yeah. He won't be there.

TOM BILLY: You drive.

MICHAEL: I'm not driving my car.

TOM BILLY: Steal a car. It's easy, I'll show you. And I won't arrest you either, this time. We'll get a Ford, I'm not sitting in a fucking Nissan for an hour with my knees knocking on my chin. If I want my teeth loosened I'll pay a dentist.

(MICHAEL unfolds a cloth and presents TOM BILLY with a Smith and Wesson snub nose.)

Nice. Do you want it back?

MICHAEL: No.

TOM BILLY: OK. Gimme some canon balls.

(MICHAEL hands over a packet of slugs from under the floorboards.)

Why do you hide this stuff? It makes it look like you're doing something wrong.

(There is a knock at the door. They freeze.)

TOM BILLY: Are you expecting anyone?

MICHAEL: No.

(The door handle turns.)

TOM BILLY: They're trying to get in.

MICHAEL: I locked it.

(TOM BILLY goes to the door listens. The rattle of keys.)

TOM BILLY: He's got a fucking key! Who's got keys?

MICHAEL: Ruairi and the Big Fellah.

(A key turns in the lock. TOM BILLY backs away from the door as COSTELLO enters and closes the door behind him. He's still in dinner jacket, but without the tie. He's not drunk.)

COSTELLO: Good evening.

(Silence.)

My speech went well. I thought. What do you think Michael?

MICHAEL: Good yeah.

TOM BILLY: *(To MICHAEL.)* Shut the fuck up!

COSTELLO: Not as many laughs as usual. But you know… circumstances. I don't want a drink thank you.

TOM BILLY: Lock that door Michael.

(MICHAEL does as he's told.)

COSTELLO: Still doing as you're told Michael?

MICHAEL: I had it locked.

COSTELLO: Looking at guns?

TOM BILLY: Yeah.

COSTELLO: This should be a job for Michael. You've done enough Tom Billy.

(COSTELLO takes his watch off, and his rings, and puts them on the side.)

This is a good watch, runs a little fast, which means you get there early. In Korea I saw an officer shoot a Gook, stoop down take the watch of the body. I didn't like that. I thought that was unAmerican. I'm serious these are gifts. Whoever. If you want them. Wedding ring. Pawn it. Buy a drink. Buy a round.

(He takes his wedding ring off, puts it on the side.)

Michael?

MICHAEL: I can't. We don't have orders.

COSTELLO: You don't get it do you Michael –

TOM BILLY: – that's what I said, I said –

COSTELLO: – shut up! –

(TOM BILLY shuts up but is not subservient in his body language.)

(To TOM BILLY.) Give him the gun.

(TOM BILLY gives MICHAEL the snub nose.)

MICHAEL: It's not what I do.

COSTELLO: You're in an army. You godda shoot the enemy. You've already killed. Hell, every dollar buys a bullet. How many dollars have you raised? I'll be in here.

(COSTELLO goes into the bathroom and closes the door.)

TOM BILLY: *(Miming.)* To the head. He'll let you. You can shut your fucking big girl eyes that way.

MICHAEL: I can't do it.

TOM BILLY: You godda. Why's it always me. You think it's easy for me? The fuck. Get in there!

(TOM BILLY virtually pushes MICHAEL into the bathroom. MICHAEL goes in. We see COSTELLO sitting on the side of the bath. TOM BILLY closes the door. TOM BILLY sits. Waits. Listens. He doesn't fret, but suddenly he stands, takes his police issue Colt and goes into the bathroom, closing the door behind him. A shot is heard.)

End of Scene.

Epilogue

(2001. The apartment. Early morning. Sun just coming up. The radio is playing Bruce Springsteen's "Born to Run". A new Bialetti bubbles. MICHAEL is cleaning his teeth in the bathroom. Hearing the Bialetti he comes out and turns it off. He is fiftyish now with a belly and a bit of grey. This station is his favourite as it plays his music – rock and punk. The DJ talks over Springsteen and fades it out. MICHAEL goes back into the bathroom and his teeth cleaning.)

DJ: The Boss reminding us that "we were born to run". 101.7 Apple FM bringing you a New York Rock and Roll sunrise! Who said you can't dance on a Tuesday morning – this is a free country! Manhattan Bridge gridlocked, Brooklyn Bridge moving slow, Holland Tunnel all clear, Lincoln tunnel all clear. Stay tuned for MTA New York City subway news. It's a beautiful bright day, look at that sky, trust me, it's September "officially temperate". Kennedy Airport, La Guardia, and Newark International report – no problems. Don't be a dummy, don't drive, use Airlink, your personal transportation system for all three airports. O456 787878 Now! We got two tickets here for Mark E Smith and the Fall November twenty fourth at the Knitting Factory, Canal Street – they're yours if you can tell me which New York rock legend was born Jeffry Ross Hyman – born 1951, died this year, 2001. Hey ho, let's go.

(The Ramones "53rd and 3rd" plays. MICHAEL comes out from the bathroom. MICHAEL laughs, and sings along. He goes into his bedroom and dresses. MICHAEL comes back dressed in his Lieutenant uniform. He takes a drink of coffee from the pot. He pours some cereal, milk, and eats it. He sits and puts on his shoes. He dresses in his FDNY coat. Time should be taken over the little things here. He sets his ansaphone. He plugs in a new gizzmo, a delayed hot pot cooker, he fiddles with some timer device on the cooker. He leaves.)

Slow To Black

The End